Beyond OODA: Developing the Orientation for Deception, Conflict and Violence

A Violence of Mind Book

ISBN xxxxxxx

Varg Freeborn

www.vargfreeborn.com

Editing by Daniel Shaw

Cover Art and Design by Lorin Michki

Formatting by Lauren Bechtel

Special thanks to Chet Richards, who offered his feedback and took the time to put his stamp of approval on my interpretations of Boyd's, and his work. That approval will forever remain a high point in my writing experience.

I would also like to thank Daniel and Lauren for their continued support of my projects, I know that hasn't always been an easy task.

Contents

Introduction

Like my first book, *Violence of Mind: Training and Preparation for Extreme Violence*, I wrote this book to fill an information gap and offer a different perspective on violence mindset. Much of what I had read or heard being talked about in the training world on the subject of violence mindset, or "combat mindset," was just desperately lacking key elements that I had experienced or observed *first-hand*.

I have shaped and refined the views expressed here based on what I have witnessed, experienced and participated in throughout my life. The thoughts I share here are my own, but I will not take credit for every concept I use since not much is new under the sun in the world of violence and combat. I simply have a less common background that allows me to develop a unique perspective on this crucial topic, and I feel compelled to share it for the good of others.

I have learned that fighters from very diverse backgrounds will often find themselves coming to similar (or the same) conclusions about how to fight or train, even though they are worlds apart in their backgrounds and experiences. There are only so many ways to be good at fighting, and human nature in force performance can be fairly predictable.

Mindset is the way you view yourself, the world around you and your position in that world at a given moment. As situations change and our environment becomes *abnormal*, reality can clash with our worldview and self-view, causing us to lose momentum in decision-making.

Orientation is what you bring to the fight, the source of all of the criteria that you use to make every decision. How you respond to emerging problems and information in real-time is based on your culture, attachments, moral values, experience, and confidence. These are the basis of what I refer to as our orientation, which forms that thing we call mindset. They control how we see ourselves and the world around us, which governs every decision we make. Your opponent has all of the same things, but his culture, experiences, and values sometimes cause him to come to different conclusions.

The biggest thing that we all seek to avoid is uncertainty since that is the nemesis of all fighters. Uncertainty is simply *white space*, a lack of answers or plans, a lack of the information needed to make a good decision. Uncertainty gets you killed. Some fill that white space with technical knowledge and training; others fill it with strong culture and values, often manifesting in extreme forms such as suicidal religious beliefs. Either way, your orientation is what fills that white space and is the most important part of determining how you will process information and make decisions in a fight.

It is also the quickest path to understanding the enemy. It is critical that you apply the two-way principle here: what governs you also governs the enemy. They have an orientation, and it is built from the same components. This enemy is most likely culturally different from you, so their orientation influences will be quite different than yours, hence why they come to different conclusions. But in general, the formula is the same.

It has been taught in warrior culture for thousands of years, "to know yourself is to know your enemy," and only through conquering yourself can you achieve victory in defeating a dedicated opponent. This book will take a deep look at building a strong orientation that can be relied upon to construct the mindset needed when facing severe adversity in combat and other forms of adversity.

Here's my disclaimer: I am not a scientist, and this book is not full of data-driven science. I caution you about the popular trend of only valuing "science" in the study of training and violence. The study of violence in the ways that we need it studied has not been done in any scientifically significant way. Violence is too widespread, too random and too often not reported, or is reported inaccurately. And let's not forget that there is no way to quantify the characteristics of a mindset reliably.

As Joseph Campbell points out in his *Pathways to Bliss*, *"You can always tell an author who is still working under the authorities by the number of footnotes he provides to his text. You must have the courage of your own belief and leave it to somebody else to verify your authority for him or herself."*

We should not discount the anecdotal evidence of the survivors or the past offenders of violence, nor should we ignore the perspectives of the participants and veterans of it who go on to become thinkers and developers in the business of violence training.

It would also be a mistake to discount my words due to my apparent lack of formal education or command of the written word. If you did, you would miss a first-hand account and a layman's analysis of the extreme violence and force performance I have seen and participated in. That participation went on for decades *before* developing and testing these concepts over years of training and teaching others in the application of force under the threat of harm or death.

I am a survivor of violence and poverty, and my lineage is generations deep in the experiences of savagery. I went on to be trained extensively as an instructor for civilians and law enforcement. I have done many of the things I will speak about in this book firsthand, and that's more than you can say for the average academic, as pretty as their prose may be. These are just my views, my *experienced* conclusions and conjecture, and I am sharing them with you for your considerations. Take it or leave it.

From the onset, I would also like to state that not all felons are predators, nor are they necessarily "bad" people. I am not characterizing an entire group in a general way. I am a felon, and I certainly would not perpetuate the *legalized discrimination* that has been leveraged against me many times in my life.

The U.S. locks up more people per capita than any other modernized country in the world. The popular estimate of the number of Americans with a felony in their past is around 20 million. It's not that hard to become a felon in the U.S., and most of you reading this have committed (or nearly committed) a felony in your lifetime; you just didn't get caught. In this work, I am discussing the specific subset of felons, and non-felons, who are dangerous to society.

I hope you find value in the pages that will follow. Any advantage you gain could be the one that saves your life or the life of someone you want to protect.

Section I

Origins: Part I

1:1. The Importance of Orientation for Mindset

The values, attachments and parameters that we use to make every decision ultimately influence our thoughts about an event. We can begin to break down those decision influencers as follows:

- Culture
- Values
- Attachments
- Parameters (internal/external)
- Experience
- Confidence
- New Information
- Genetics

To study the "martial arts" of gunfighting, edged weapons, grappling and striking while ignoring the study of orientation, implicit guidance, and information analysis and synthesis is to ignore mindset as a whole. Does the individual fighter or soldier necessarily need to have an academic level education on the deep nuances of these concepts to be effective? No. But trainers, instructors, educators and administrators of the programs that train and prepare these men and women not only better have an understanding of it, but their programs must be built around the deep development of these concepts.

You can have every young man screaming, "Marines make blood flow! Blood makes the grass grow!" for months before sending them into war. However, suppose their values, cultural inputs, experiences, fears and attachments were not addressed. In that case, you will have men freeze and possibly retreat or hide when presented with the opportunity to be on the losing end of that "make the blood flow" activity. The implicit guidance of the underlying factors in decision-making must be shaped to influence decision-making under force pressure that is intuitive and has the element of speed as an advantage on one's behalf.

The same is true of everyone else training to prepare for extreme violence on any level. Training physical skills and strength and repeating the mantra, "I train, so I am harder to kill!" doesn't necessarily make you harder to kill. Your decision-making under pressure will have much more to do with your outcomes in a deadly confrontation than how much you can bench press or deadlift or how fast you can shoot or submit someone on your back.

To reach reliable effectiveness through proper orientation guidance, it is required for individual operators and organizations to be specifically prepared for it. Even ancient militaries and violence training cultures were not ignorant of this, which gives us ages-old meditations like *"memento mori,"* encouraging the warrior to contemplate and be comfortable with his own death.

This was ancient man's way of exhibiting that he was aware of the implicit guidance and potential biases of one's fears, beliefs, experiences and attachments directly to his well-being and secondarily to those he cares about and will leave behind. They understood how important it was for battle effectiveness to have these fears and attachments sorted out in a way as to not prohibit appropriate and swift decision-making in battle.

In my pursuit to understand what makes some so effective and efficient in decision-making during the pressure of deadly force, I realized that the mindset, which I later recognized as the orientation, is the foundation for these capabilities. I learned this after living through a few decades of household violence, criminal violence and prison, and then entering the world of professional violence training. I realized two things: First, being trained to a highly proficient level does not guarantee that the individual will perform well under force pressure. Second, the lack of training does not guarantee that the individual will not perform well under force pressure.

Many of the most dangerous people I have known who touted dramatic success records in deadly force encounters were criminals armed only with their experiences and orientation as preparation. Yet, they repeatedly performed at a very high level under mortal threat. These were gangbangers and criminals, many of them barely out of their teens. One kid in particular that I recall from prison had been shot eleven times in four separate shooting incidents. What do you think was embedded deep in his orientation that would assist him in clear decision-making during a deadly fight? Confidence from successful experience? A lack of fear from being a high-rate survivor? Strategies and procedures developed from the real-time experience he gained? These are the questions we will explore in this book to understand what builds the most efficient and deadly violent minds.

1:2. Beyond Boyd

This book is not about Col. John Boyd. I seriously considered omitting any mention of Boyd and his concepts just to avoid the inevitable event that someone, somewhere, will get stuck on the "Boyd" part and miss the message of the book completely.

Boyd devotees get pretty riled up when someone interprets the O.O.D.A. (Observe, Orient, Decide, Act) and Boyd's other work differently than they do. It has ruined many discussions for me already. I concluded, however, that it would be impossible to lay out my concept of orientation and mindset without establishing where my inspirations came from, how I developed the concept, and how I believe it to be an interpretive extension of what Boyd left us. Therefore, while I do not feel like this is wholly interpretive of his work, I credit him with the inspiration to pursue this concept and to study it retrospectively across all of my experiences.

No one knows for sure what Boyd meant with many of his concepts because he never truly elaborated on them in written or recorded form beyond a few published papers (that one could argue Boyd himself never viewed as finished). If you did not work directly with him or attend one of his presentations, you likely will never hear an accurate expansion of Boyd's concepts. He never wrote a book or recorded any public video (though a few low-quality recordings of him exist). He wrote a few small pieces, but they seem to be written more as guide notes for his presentations, where he would then expand upon them in person. Nevertheless, "experts" everywhere love to expound upon how much they understand the O.O.D.A. Loop and what Boyd "actually meant." Most often, they are just incorrect.

Similarly, I will not address Boyd's Aerial Attack Study (1964) at all. It has very little to do with the subject matter here, and I am only interested in Boyd's later work, where he developed the concept of orientation more deeply. In my opinion, the AAS was part of the early groundwork, but the highly refined and more thoroughly developed concepts came in the three full decades of his work that followed the AAS. (If you are interested in an overview of Boyd's framework, I recommend Chet Richards' book *Certain to Win*. Boyd himself reviewed the early drafts, and Richards circulated the later revisions for comments by Boyd's other associates.)

But at the least, I owe Boyd for the very word "orientation" and the inspiration of its meaning in my understanding and teachings about combat mindset and mindset in general. It was through my study of the O.O.D.A. concept and comparing it to my own real experience in deadly violence and other fast-moving situations that I came to realize the importance and genius behind that second "O."

Boyd clearly stated in his paper, *Organic Design for Command and Control*:

> *"Orientation is the Schwerpunkt. It shapes the way we interact with the environment—hence orientation shapes the way we observe, the way we decide, the way we act. In this sense, orientation shapes the character of present observation-orientation-decision-action loops--while these present loops shape the character of future orientation.*
>
> *The second O, orientation—as the repository of our genetic heritage, cultural tradition and previous experiences—is the most essential part of the O.O.D.A. loop since it shapes the way we observe, the way we decide, the way we act. "*

I could simply stop with that quote from Boyd and be completely justified in my assertions about orientation in relation to what Boyd intended the orientation concept to be. He clearly states that orientation is the most important component of the loop concept because it shapes the way we observe, decide and act. But we will do it a much better justice and look to more clues that will tie the concepts together and show why the average and common interpretations of the O.O.D.A. loop fall way short of extracting the actual value from it.

Since high-stress situations, such as deadly fights, require strong and rapid decision-making, it becomes very evident that what you bring to the fight is your orientation and its inputs. Everything else: observation, decision-making, and acting all occur during the moment. Those *in-the-fight* elements can be prepared for with physical fitness, conditioning, and training in skills, techniques and procedures. But what you truly bring *to* the fight is your orientation, and this also can be shaped and trained consciously to a high degree.

Suppose we understand that orientation becomes the foundation of mindset, the basis for all decision-making. In that case, it stands to reason that if we want to shape a stronger mindset for some particularly challenging task like combat or deadly fighting, we must first shape the elements that make up our orientation. Once this orientation is brought into line with the likely decisions we will have to make in a competitive situation, we can create that intuitive bond between decision-making criteria and our skill sets and procedures.

This results in one's ability to develop an intuitive understanding of high-speed combat and violence problems. Intuitive recognition and decision-making can become nearly autonomous within the mind, significantly speeding up the decision-act process. The intuitive mind understands the problems at hand without much conscious thought and then selects decisions from a pre-selected group of possible choices. Boyd referred to this as "implicit guidance." Before we go deeper into that, let's look at Boyd's concept of O.O.D.A. directly.

1:3. O.O.D.A.

I am not alone in my views of Boyd's orientation component. His colleagues, including the few who worked directly with him to develop many of these concepts, also seem to agree with this interpretation. But it doesn't appear to be how the average person interprets it. The way that many people understand Boyd's O.O.D.A. loop is as follows:

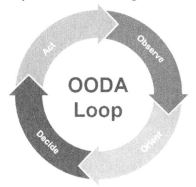

Observe - Orient - Decide - Act

That's it. Unfortunately, that leaves *a lot* to interpretation. I have even witnessed it being taught with the "orient" component referring to "physically orienting yourself to the threat," which could not be more incorrect. If you believe any version of the Loop's interpretation that even resembles this model, you are missing the mark wholesale. "Orient" does not denote a physical act, nor does it describe a decision. I venture a guess that a great majority of people who are teaching or talking about O.O.D.A. have not studied Boyd, Boyd's briefings in his own words, nor the work of Boyd's colleagues who worked directly with him on these concepts.

In truth, what the O.O.D.A. concept essentially means, is that your observation feeds your orientation, and your orientation drives your decision-making. That is a foundational premise. The recognition (which is observation) triggers your orientation upon which all decisions

15

are based. This exposes a major flaw in most combat or fight training because styles, systems, methods and instructors are hell-bent on the repetition and development of physical skills while mostly ignoring the root sources of decision making in the trainee.

And while some training is designed to build "mental toughness," it is not addressing true mindset development and the preparation for proper decision making because it is not addressing the orientation components responsible for the information our decisions are based upon. One of the ways this is evidenced is by the frequent occurrence of highly trained law enforcement officers making use of force mistakes that end in policy violations, lawsuits and criminal charges, or they end with the officer being maimed or killed as a result of the poor decisions they made during the fight. Simply developing physical capabilities, mental toughness and being "ready to fight" is not preparing you to make precise, effective and efficient decisions about very specific problems under force pressure. We see the sad results of this approach nearly every day on our streets and on our battlefields.

1:4. Boyd's Colleagues and the Development of O.O.D.A.

Two people who worked very closely with Boyd are Chuck Spinney and Chet Richards. They have gone forth and produced a lot of literature about Boyd's various concepts, providing a tremendous amount of insight into them. Richards and Spinney both worked with Boyd on many of his writings and continued to work with him well past Boyd's military days.

In 2012, Richards published '*Boyd's O.O.D.A. Loop*' for J. Addams and Partners, a private company. His paper offered an application of the O.O.D.A. in a business context for private corporations. Richards clearly states that Boyd did create the complex graphic of the multi-looping, orientation-centered O.O.D.A. pictured below, despite that graphic often being incorrectly credited to Spinney.

We know this is true because Chuck Spinney also directly credits Boyd with the same graphic, explaining how the diagram was developed as a "joint effort in the late 1980's" between Spinney, Richards and Boyd himself, which Spinney expands upon in his paper, *Evolutionary Epistemology: A Personal View of John Boyd's Destruction and Creation and it's centrality to the O.O.D.A. Loop*. This is a profound revelation

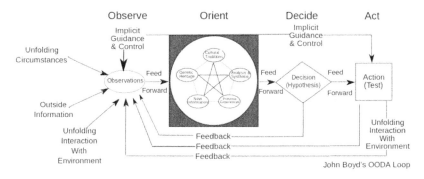

John Boyd's OODA Loop

17

because it validates that Boyd had developed O.O.D.A. beyond the simple process most, unfortunately, know it as.

Robert Coram also offers an excellent explanation of O.O.D.A. in his book *"Boyd, The Fighter Pilot Who Changed the Art of War,"*

"Understanding the O.O.D.A. Loop is difficult. First, even though it is called a "loop," it is not. A drawing of the Loop shows thirty arrows connecting the various ingredients, which means hundreds of possible "loops" can be derived. The best drawing of the O.O.D.A. Loop was done by Spinney [which Spinney credits Boyd for] for Boyd's briefings. It shows a considerable orientation part of the cycle. Becoming oriented to a competitive situation means bringing to bear the cultural traditions, genetic heritage, new information, previous experiences, and analysis/synthesis process of the person doing the orienting -- a complex integration that each person does differently. These human differences make the Loop unpredictable. In addition, the orientation phase is a nonlinear feedback system, which, by its very nature, means this is a pathway to the unknown. The unpredictability is crucial to the success of the O.O.D.A. Loop.

Only three arrows are on the main axis, and these are what most see when they look at the Observe > Orient > Decide > Act cycle. But this linear understanding and its common result -- an attempt to use the Loop mechanically -- is not at all what Boyd had in mind."

This is also an interesting take on the O.O.D.A. that it is the unpredictability that makes it successful. In *Violence of Mind*, I talk about how unpredictability is both the greatest deterrent and a key component to fighting success. But unpredictability is nearly impossible to fake; it has to be an organic result of the O.O.D.A. process and one that comes from a well-developed orientation in particular.

Conversely, a fighter with a well-developed orientation for force pressure performance will often develop the ability to predict the opponent's moves quite accurately, especially if that opponent is not as well developed as they are in perception and analysis/synthesis.

1:5. The Application of the O.O.D.A. in Real-Time Decision Making

Chet Richards describes how Boyd evolved his concepts to be centered around the orientation complex and how it affected real-time decision-making. He explains how the original, circular and simple O.O.D.A. *"did not work well when one is engaged with an opponent."* Of course, this implies that the new loop configuration, being centered around the orient component, directly addressed the problems of decision-making "when one is engaged." In other words, *real-time application of decision-making during an engagement*, a problem he specifically points out, was not addressed in the original, simpler O.O.D.A.

According to Richards in his paper "Boyd's O.O.D.A. Loop," published in the Norwegian Defense Journal, Necesse, March 2020, 142-165:

"To get a handle on it, begin with the centrality of orientation and imagine that when we are engaged with opponents—or in the case of business, with competitors and customers—our actions will flow from it implicitly, that is, without explicit (e.g., written or detailed verbal) commands or instructions, most of the time. Orientation is an ancient idea embodied in the concept of mindfulness, but it is as modern as fighter pilots who talk about maintaining "situation awareness."

Richards notes that the concept of "implicit guidance" differentiates the earlier, circular and simpler version of the O.O.D.A. loop from the more complex, orientation-centered O.O.D.A. loop and

Boyd's constant emphasis on orientation for implicit guidance for the express purpose of real-time decision making. Richards continues:

"For the same reason, initiating actions via the circular O.O.D.A. loop does not work well when one is engaged with an opponent. The need to go through stages before coming around to action is too slow, as Storr observed, and too easy to disrupt (Klein, 1999). If, on the other hand, action can flow rapidly from orientation directly via an implicit guidance and control (IG&C) link, then any pattern of actions becomes possible. In particular, abrupt shifts, which Boyd (1986) called "asymmetric fast transients," from cheng to ch'i, are straightforward. Just fire the ch'i when the time is right. The jarring transition jerks opponents off-balance mentally (sometimes physically) and sets them up for the exploitation to follow."

Being a student of martial studies for a few decades now leaves me bewildered how anyone who also claims to be a student of it cannot extrapolate the essence of "action flowing rapidly from orientation directly via an implicit guidance and control." In other words, it should be apparent that there is a real-time application of orientation components through observe-decide-act, which sometimes occurs at an unconscious level directly from orient to act. This understanding runs in a continuous stream throughout thousands of years of writings on the subject. Any serious study of Musashi, Sun Tzu, Bushido, and Boyd will reveal the said consistency.

As Richards continues,

"One of Boyd's favorite strategists, the 17th-century samurai Miyamoto Musashi (trans. 1982), whose Book of Five Rings is still studied in both military and business schools, observed that such transients would produce a period, though perhaps only a moment, of confusion, hesitation, surprise, even debilitating shock and disorientation. During that period, when the opponent does not have an accurate understanding

of the situation or the ability to formulate a coherent concept for dealing with it, we can act with little fear of effective counteraction. For this reason, some strategists, including the commentators on Sun Tzu, the Japanese of the samurai period, and Boyd in our day, have raised the study of cheng/ch'i to the level of art."

I agree that Boyd deserves his place among Sun Tzu and Musashi as great martial strategists. I also believe that they are all saying essentially the same thing, in finer grades of detail. Nothing is new under the sun—only our perception changes with time and understanding.

1:6. Adaptability and Agility, the Ancient Wisdom of Orientation

I was once asked in a class to narrow my personal "philosophy" down to just one word. This was a gunfighting instructor development course at a law enforcement training facility, so the context was heavily centered around fighting. Still, the question was intentionally broad enough to include our philosophy about life as well.

Since a personal philosophy would be a set of principles that guides one through life's decisions and outlook, I nailed my one-word philosophy down to adaptability. There is not one other guiding principle that I can think of that would overpower its importance in fighting, relationships, business, and life. It's not always the physically fastest who wins in combat; it's often the one who adapts *and demonstrates mental agility* in the situation more thoroughly. (We'll not perpetuate any rampant misquotations of Darwin here, but we should understand that adaptability is a mandatory characteristic for survival in an evolutionary sense as well.) But adaptability by itself is never enough to gain control.

As Boyd stated in *Organic Design for Command and Control*, adaptability is an essential component of both dealing with a changing environment and remaining unpredictable in actions:

"Adaptability implies variety and rapidity. Without variety and rapidity, one can neither be unpredictable nor cope with changing and unforeseen circumstances."

He went into great detail regarding destructive deduction and creative induction as processes that allow an individual (or, equally, an organization) to deal with a rapidly changing environment. Boyd also evolved this concept further, according to Richards, referencing a note from Boyd dated August 18, 1992:

"If we're only adapting, we're in the perpetual catch-up mode. He [the opponent] has the initiative."

We must understand that adaptability without agility leaves us in a reactionary mode, which is not where you want to be in a fight or any other strategic situation. Adaptability gives us variety, while agility gives us rapidity, and that combination is how we shift initiative and apply pressure rather than simply responding to pressure. I understand this from an experiential perspective, there is no other way to get ahead of the opponent reliably, and it has to become a part of your entire orientation foundationally.

In *'The Conceptual Spiral'* (1992), Boyd also stated,

"While we can comprehend and predict some portions of the ever-changing world that unfolds before us, other portions seem forever indistinct and unpredictable."

"Since survival and growth are directly connected with the uncertain, ever-changing, unpredictable world of winning and losing, we will exploit this whirling conceptual spiral of orientation, mismatches, analysis/synthesis, reorientation, mismatches, analysis/synthesis...so that we can comprehend, cope with, and shape--as well as be shaped by--that world and the novelty that arises out of it."

This is an incredibly insightful look at the process of orientation and re-orientation, all resulting in adaptability and the systematic increase in chances of the prediction of outcomes. Can one conclude that none of this happens in *real time*?

To be clear, I am not arguing that anyone should enter into any conflict without pre-planned responses whatsoever. That would be ridiculous and negate all of the time we spend on the range, at the gym, in the ring, or on the mat. Since orientation is a pre-existing condition of O.O.D.A. (at least in part), it stands to reason that a planning/preparatory phase is both possible and necessary to develop it. Boyd referred to these pre-planned responses and options are our "repertoire," which gives us flexibility even within our implicit guidance and control link. This can happen by circumstance, like the youth born into violent and chaotic environments or by intention through training and pressure inoculation.

It's quite simple; being dogmatic and inflexible in fighting (and in life) will often cause failure. By being open-minded in your observation, flexible in your approach, and adaptable (with agility) in your actions, you are more likely to be successful at most tasks that involve complex problem solving and strategic positioning.

The importance of orientation in real-time decision-making is universal. Suppose one's orientation to the situation is not in place and appropriate. In that case, one will not be able to utilize any acquired physical skills for lack of being able to apply proper decision-making in the moment. Even having a pre-planned counter-attack that could play out perfectly with the adversary's attack pattern would be no good whatsoever if the person wanting to counter-attack did not have the components of orientation in place (cultural, genetic, experience, etc.) that were supportive of making the decision to utilize the pre-planned counter-attack.

This is a complex way of saying that you need the skills, techniques and procedures to win, the willingness and confidence (orientation) to perform them, and the ability to analyze and synthesize new information to modify as necessary (adaptability and agility), to perform at an efficient level when faced with an attack. In addition to this, to become highly proficient and more rapid than the opponent, the actor must have a well-developed implicit guidance and command link in place, allowing them to cue action strictly off of observation while bypassing the other decision-making loops normally used in that process

1:7. Observation, Analysis and Synthesis

According to Boyd, there are two ways to process incoming information: analysis and synthesis. As he elaborated on extensively in his *Creation and Destruction* paper, he believed that one could analyze information coming in by looking at it in components and drawing conclusions through deduction. Boyd explained that we can also synthesize information by taking different components and sometimes unrelated pieces of information, both from outside and inside of us, synthesizing them into a new whole information set. Boyd believed to reach a creativity level, one had to enact a destructive process to clear the way for the creative process.

David Eagleman, a modern neuroscientist specializing in creativity, points out that humans spend an enormous amount of time thinking about "what if's" and "what could have been's," as he puts it. He contends that we spend our cognitive processes primarily in three main operations: bending, breaking and blending. This, I would argue, is precisely what Boyd talks about and refers to as analysis and synthesis.

Another example comes from none other than Steve Jobs, speaking of the creative process in his famous "lost interview,"

"Designing a product is keeping 5,000 things in your brain, these concepts, and fitting them all together and kind of continuing to push to fit them together in new and different ways to get what you want. And every day, you discover something new, that is a new problem or a new opportunity, to fit these things together a little differently."

In other words, you are constantly bringing in new information, and synthesizing it in new ways, often through the destruction of some old information or way of thinking. The examples are endless: *"synthesis," "thinking outside of the box," "blending, breaking and bending,"* etc. No matter how you refer to it, it is how we, as humans reach the point of creativity, and we do it through implicit guidance based on our orientation.

Analysis and synthesis is the process of creativity. My position here is that creativity is absolutely needed for problem-solving and that fighting and violence are indeed extreme exercises in problem-solving, whether it is at the large organizational level or the one-on-one interpersonal level.

Think of it like this: Let's say that you had some training in which you were attacked by a knife-wielding assailant. In that scenario, you first tried to turn and run away, which resulted in you being overtaken and stabbed multiple times. When you were again faced by the same attacker approaching in the same way, you now had this new information to synthesize with the familiar information you were seeing in front of you, the attacker. You didn't try to run because you learned that response wouldn't work, yet you still did not have a definite answer. You begin to get creative and try to reach for the knife arm, but you reach too high up and again get stabbed a few times.

Round three comes, and now you have even more information to try to use to problem solve. Same attacker, same approach, but this time you use some deception, perhaps feigning to run because you know it will draw him in, but you turn in and then clamp down with both hands near the wrist of the knife hand and isolate it away from him and his other hand. You became creative in real-time because you had enough information inside your orientation, your *experiences* specifically, to synthesize the information coming in to create a solution and a subsequent action.

The problem with violence is that we don't really get the chance to practice and gain real experiences in a way that doesn't truly endanger us. We can only get close through the type of mock force-on-force training that I am speaking of above. And without the specific type of experience, plus the retrospective understanding of the experience, one can not foster this process in students, cops or soldiers.

It can not be taught; it can only be *caused* to happen in the student's mind. This is because it is not a linear problem. Therefore simply learning singular martial arts defenses or fighting moves will not prepare the individual for this decision-making *analysis and synthesis* part of the process. Suppose you take the knife attacker drill detailed above, and instead of three evolutions, you had given the student a repeated drill on the two-handed wrist grab with a compliant partner. Would they have gotten it right on their first evolution with a non-compliant attacker? Maybe. But at best, they would have missed a very important developmental process along the way. They would have missed the analysis and synthesis part of the first two evolutions, which caused them to reach true creativity and thus begin to achieve *adaptability*. For that matter, the student may even think of something you have not. This is how it all ties together.

Robbing students, police cadets and future soldiers of that process of *analysis and synthesis through doing* is a leading cause of inaccurate attitudes that graduates have about their own capabilities. It is a disservice from instructors and teachers. Perhaps I am biased towards this type of learning because I learned violence by being thrown into a violent world at a young age and then tossed into the adult penitentiary as a teenager to learn the hard way. Humans learn well by doing. The bad part is that street violence, prison, and war are high casualty environments that claim a lot of lives along the way.

What we can do for our students, future cops, and soldiers is to give them prolonged processes to work through and learn from, including allowing them to have some failures. While I don't allow my students playing a "good guy" role to lay down and "die" in force-on-force classes, I do allow them to fail and get shot with simulated ammunition *a lot*. They often know they would have died if the bullets were real, and it's critical to the process that they know this. It raises the importance of the information in their orientation, which drives it harder to look for implicit guidance links that will be reliable under rapid force pressure.

In cases like mine, the average violent criminal's experience, we are put through violent and life-threatening events without any formal prior preparation. This creates a strong feedback loop within our orientation that drives a robust analysis and synthesis system within our decision-making process. A similar thing happens to young soldiers sent to war with minimal preparation for the violence they will face. This is also true for some cops in certain high-violence jurisdictions.

So if learning by doing is the best way to entrench our orientation with a highly developed analysis and synthesis feedback loop, why not just throw new fighters out into the wild and let them find their way? I think we all see how that ends up for the "high risk" youth of violent environments and for the morally injured and psychologically battered war veterans who return home a few short years later completely and thoroughly changed so severely that they haven't had time to adjust to their new orientation or deal with its consequences.

In that sense, the at-risk youth are probably better off since they have often had violence exposure starting at a very young age, progressively having been inoculated to its ill effects over time. The cop or soldier, conversely, gets a "culture shock" to their orientation, in which all of their internal changes happen in a very short period. It's quite honestly a lot for the human mind to bear. I also speculate that this shorter process does not produce the same robustness in their orientation, specifically in the analysis and synthesis component of decision-making.

So, we have much to think about in terms of understanding our perceptions of the world around us and what goes into our process of making decisions about dealing with it. I advocate for longer processes and deeper understanding to take priority over physical skills and simple "mental toughness" drills.

1:8. Incestuous Amplification

If you've read my previous work, *Violence of Mind*, you'll have read about my teaching concept: *"stop looking for things and start looking at things."* I use a lot of examples to bring this concept home in the mind's of the students. One such example is the highly predictable actor in close quarters or shoothouse training that inevitably shoots a hostage, bystander or police target upon entering a room.

Looking at the "target" clearly indicates no weapon is present, often including other clear visuals like cell phones or badges. Without fail, the actor goes in and reacts not to what is in front of them but what they *think* is in front of them. They turned the corner expecting to see a bad guy, which is partially what they should do, but they acted on seeing a bad guy when there was not one there. They failed to positively identify their target before reacting with deadly force. Why does this and many other common mismatches between reality and perception happen?

One explanation comes from Chuck Spinney, *incestuous amplification*. Mr. Spinney explains this well in his blog post, *Iraq Invasion Anniversary: Inside The Decider's Head* (22 March 2013),

"Incestuous Amplification...occurs when the preconceptions in the decider's Orientation (that is, his/her repository of ideology, belief systems, cultural heritage, previous experiences, education, genetic heritage, etc.) misshape the Observations feeding that Orientation.

Note that the keyword is misshape: there is no question that one's Orientation always shapes everything that is apprehended in the environment or that one's orientation evolves and changes over time in response to changes in the interaction between the observing organism and its environment.

A six-year-old sees the world very differently than when he is 60. The relevant measure of merit is whether that evolving Orientation produces Decisions and Actions that improve the match-up between the decision-making organism and its environment as it marches along the one-way arrow of time.

But when the decider's Orientation becomes infected by Incestuous Amplification, the opposite occurs — his or her Orientation distorts observations in a way that drives the interaction toward an ever-increasing mismatch between the organism and its environment."

Chet Richards expands on this by explaining the relationship between orientation and observation in his Slightly East of New blog post *Incestuous Delusion* (August 4, 2013)

"What we're talking about, then, is the (incestuous) relationship in the O.O.D.A. "loop" between Observation and Orientation. Observation is the only feed into Orientation, but Orientation also implicitly guides and controls Observation. It is so tempting in some people and organizations for Orientation to steer Observation so that only agreeable facts, data, and other input are observed, and Orientation itself possesses enormous powers to interpret contradictory information in ways that actually reinforce existing beliefs and mindsets."

To tie this all together, we begin to clearly understand the role that our orientation plays in our decision making, the role that observation plays in feeding our orientation new information to synthesize, and how that feedback loop can become isolated, obstructed or corrupted, causing mismatches between what we are seeing and what is actually happening around us. These mismatches will eventually manifest themselves as failure when the environment imposes its reality upon us.

As Richards says, ***"Observation is the only feed into Orientation, but Orientation also implicitly guides and controls Observation."*** He means that in the moment of battle, or the moment of decisiveness, the only thing pushing into orientation is that which we are observing. Our interpretation of that observed information (and of ourselves and our place in the world) is of utmost importance in the quality of the decisions that come forth from that process. That interpretation is based entirely on our orientation and its clarity.

1:9. Beyond Boyd and O.O.D.A.

In the rest of this book, I will attempt to break down in detail and in layman's terms how some of these problems arise and how to fix them in our preparations and training. I hope this section helped you understand the complexity that truly exists within John Boyd's O.O.D.A. concept and how important the component of orientation really is. And trust me, it goes much deeper than we are daring to dive here. I only sought to establish the origins of some of the terminology and concepts I share on these matters to lay the foundations of what we will be discussing for the remainder of this book. This is not intended to be a study or exhaustive interpretation of O.O.D.A. (For more along those lines, you can look to all of the sources I cited.) You'll notice I spent a lot of time on the orientation and not on the other letters. Because this is not about the O.O.D.A., and frankly, I don't find it particularly useful for my purposes. The orientation is what matters, it is obviously what Boyd thought to be the most critical part, and that is where I have focused my time developing the concepts around how I see it.

This book is, in fact, a presentation of *my* understanding of how to construct a mindset suited for violence, combat, interpersonal conflict, competition, business and life. It's a retrospective look back into my experiences with violence, extreme events and extreme people. It is also a well-thought-out look at how to examine what naturally happens for some people, then using that information to create processes for others to benefit from similar results in robust decision-making capabilities.

Origins: Part II

1:10. Experience, Culture and Values

The second part of the origins of the concepts and perspectives in this book comes from my own experiences, culture and values (especially from the first 25 years of my life). I outlined my past in some detail in *Violence of Mind*, so I won't do a complete retelling here. However, for the sake of readers who started with this book, I will briefly illustrate how my views on violence, orientation, concealment, criminal behavior and conflict were shaped by experience.

I am not an academic or a licensed professional who has merely studied these topics or worked in a field in close proximity to extreme adversity, violence and conflict. I lived it and participated in it. Born to a 16-year-old mother, I grew up in a drug house full of extreme violence. Nearly all of my aunts and uncles also lived there throughout that time, and with them came drug abuse, alcohol abuse, domestic abuse, violence and even murder. Most of my family were outright criminals, a few were gang members, and many of the men were ex-cons who had done extensive time in prison.

This led to a teen life that was quite tragic and scarred with drugs, alcohol and violence. Several family members suffered young deaths from overdoses or having been murdered. I even discovered the body of an uncle who overdosed lying against his apartment door. I had to push his body across the floor with the door to get it open enough so I could slide through the opening and over top of his purple corpse.

By the time I was a teen, I had already witnessed, and at times been a victim of, extreme violence and beatings. I was even the intended victim of a stabbing attack when I was around seven years old but was lucky enough to be saved by an uncle who came home just in time (the same uncle I later found dead).

To say I was a rough kid would be an understatement. It's not that I didn't want a better life, I tried to be creative and productive, but the support and opportunity just weren't in the cards for me.

At age 18, I found myself the target of a vicious attack, to which I responded by stabbing the main guy two dozen times. A month after turning 19 years old, I was sentenced to five years in the adult penitentiary system. I was a 135lbs teenage kid entering the brutal world of prison life in the U.S. penal system. Again, this isn't a biography, so I won't go into the wonderful details. However, throughout the book, I will use my experiences to add color to the concepts presented here and tell stories that will give anecdotal evidence supporting them.

I served the entire five years, and it was brutal. More so psychologically than physically, but there was a strong continuous dose of both for my young mind during the entire time. The system is ruthless, the inmates are viciously brutal, and the experience shapes the minds of young men in a way that quite literally nothing else can, and it does so by the millions each year. Frankly, it is a shockingly thorough and efficient training program that constructs impenetrable orientations within mostly criminal minds. I *grew up* there, within those walls and within those very specific cultural constraints that completely rewire whatever you thought you knew and believed in previous to landing there.

Beginning with my upbringing in a culture that glorified violence and embraced criminally selective values, into my adolescence where I participated in much of it, and throughout my transition into adulthood inside of the brutal world of prison, my orientation was thoroughly shaped to accept, master and demonstrate everything I will talk about in this book. These aren't concepts I developed in a classroom or for a thesis on a graduate-level project. They result from me reverse-engineering what I experienced or witnessed and analyzing it to find ways to help good, non-criminally minded people absorb and learn from it. And it isn't just about what I experienced out *in the wild*, either.

42

1:11. Training and Development

Upon my release from prison, I went right to work, trying to do things the "right way," at least as best as I could figure out what the "right way" was. I was very fortunate to petition the courts for a restoration of my rights, which included a relief of disability from owning firearms. By a miracle, I was granted all of that. I was eventually able to hold public office, vote, sit on a jury, and own and possess firearms. I can pass a NICS check, though I am still literally a felon. It's complicated but very true. I am one of the very few violent felons able to do so.

I pursued training in violence and self-defense and was again very fortunate to get pulled deep into the world of law enforcement training. My eventual work in the gun industry allowed me access to many law enforcement-only, closed enrollment training opportunities. I have attended law enforcement Breaching School for thermal, ballistic and mechanical breaching. I have trained with some of the best in the world in law enforcement close protection detail work, including the driving and caravan components.

I've logged hundreds and hundreds of hours in shoothouses training with top instructors in both military and law enforcement on CQB (close quarters battle) and high-risk warrant service and room entry, all the way to me being certified as a CQB instructor up to full-team SWAT standards through a law enforcement training facility, where I remain a guest cadre instructor to this day. For several years, I have also been a guest cadre instructor for my former home state's Tactical Officer's Association, teaching at one of the nation's largest police training conventions.

I trained in gunfighting and gunfight instruction with many great shooters and conflict tacticians for over a decade. I spent some of those same years in and out of boxing and grappling gyms, learning as much as I could about how to end fights decisively and quickly. For roughly a dozen years, I operated my own training company teaching law enforcement and civilians how to prepare for and effectively deal with the ultra-violent predator.

It's important to note that even though I had been involved in a tremendous amount of violence and participated in weapon-based violence both on the streets and in prison, I still sought out information and training in all of it from instructors with legitimate experience that differed from my own. I wanted to understand the mistakes I had made that had gotten me into so much trouble. I also wanted to understand the problems of violence as deeply as possible so that I could bring a truly experienced perspective to others and help them avoid those losses as well.

Among the most valuable of my experiences has been the force-on-force training classes that I conduct. Using Glocks converted to fire-simulated ammunition, the same equipment that the military and law enforcement use, I design simulation scenarios putting students into complicated, complex or chaotic situations. Sometimes it is a simple robbery; other times, it is group or mob violence. Sometimes someone they care about is involved and requires protection; other times, they are alone. In all of them, they are forced to make high-stakes decisions in compressed times under extreme stress.

After several years of running this type of training, I am able to observe patterns of behavior emerge. People tend to make a handful of the same mistakes. Although individuals are very different in how those mistakes are manifested, there are more similarities than differences across the board.

It's also quite revealing to watch people's skills degrade under pressure and threat when those specific skills were highly developed prior to that event. These are people who have repeatedly demonstrated that they could reliably perform skills like drawing, shooting and weapon manipulations on the square range, and sometimes for years on end prior to showing up to force-on-force training. Then, when facing the threat of force and being shot at (even though it is a simulation, it is scary and does have some pain consequence), they begin to lose control, and their skills degrade to subpar levels of performance if not outright failures. Tasks such as shooting accuracy at close distances, drawing a gun from a holster, or clearing a malfunction become difficult or impossible. They forget the proper steps or just rush through everything, causing their failures. Boyd pointed out how this is not only predictable but also usable against an opponent, *"Unless such menacing pressure is relieved, adversary will experience various combinations of uncertainty, doubt, confusion, self-deception, indecision, fear, panic, discouragement, despair…"* (Strategic Game, 44). As Boyd, Musashi, Sun Tzu, and many others have repeatedly said: *if something is bad, the basic idea is to give the opponent as much of it as possible while minimizing it in yourself.*

I have observed people crumble in fear, not being able to fight back as they are overwhelmed with the force coming at them, while others who have less training stand and fight and often win! Because I have observed and participated in a lot of violence in my life, I have observed people in real situations previous to these training experiences. I have even seen individuals killed while noticing how others responded to the scenes. I can say that there are many similarities between the real events and the training simulations, at least in how I run them. Bringing that real experience with me into force-on-force training allows me to both design scenarios to solicit certain decision-making responses and give me a chance to recreate or notice similar responses that I have observed in real-life situations.

This experience in its totality creates a data set that, while not exactly quantifiable, allows me to identify common problems and work to find solutions to them, largely by looking backward and determining how I or others I observed were able to do it. In all of my experiences, both real and in training, I have found that one's orientation and subsequent mental functions will dictate all of his or her perspectives, perceptions, decisions and actions. I learned that past performance in the absence of stress is NOT an indicator of performance under stress and that this is also heavily affected by orientation. Conversely, I have watched several instances of completely inexperienced and untrained people performing exceptionally well in both training and real events. How can we possibly understand such seemingly random results? The answers lie within our perception of the problems, and within the stories, we tell ourselves about the world around us and how we fit into it.

Section II:

Operating Inward

2:1. Mythos: The Stories We Tell Ourselves

"One could--as I have--define a ritual as an opportunity to participate directly in a myth."
-Joseph Campbell

The self-defense community, gun community, law enforcement, and military communities are chock full of imagery and mythos from warrior culture. From the pirate patches of some special operations units to the Spartan helmets machined into the AR-15 lowers of plain civilians, the imagery of the Spartan life, the Viking warrior and the Samurai are so heavily commercialized that it's a wonder that they have any meaning left at all. But it can not be denied that symbolism is ultra-powerful to the human psyche and can be useful when applied *correctly* (not commercialized and diluted).

I have always found it odd that the Spartan became the hero archetype for so many modern "warriors." In most archetypal inspirations of the hero type, the hero was victorious in some final battle, and we all know that's not how it ended for the Spartans. The glorification of the valor and courage in the movie *The 300* is possibly responsible for much of this. But I do *get it*. The Spartans were a war society. Boys began training around age seven, and by age 20, they became full-time soldiers.

The "Spartan life," as it is called, is one of training and discipline, of a readiness to go to war, and something in the spirit of many modern men clamor for this sort of mythos. It is quite necessary for these men to have something to both inspire them and to identify with at the same time, especially those that have chosen a profession that takes them into danger, such as law enforcement or the military.

But our modernized culture has taken this away from modern man. It continues to work hard to strip away the last traces of warrior mythos from him at a fundamentally cultural level. Even men's razor companies now run ads encouraging men to fight "toxic masculinity," encouraging them to be compassionate and soft. This, *on its face*, is a good cause, but it is one that many believe is ultimately part of a more significant societal attack on the strong male persona.

Once again, we enter into an era where the warrior is no longer admired or wanted by the mainstream. There's a war on guns, a war on self-defense, and a war on strong masculinity. But, much like gun control, this only serves to strip the law-abiding of their mythos and masculinity. The counterculture of the criminal world will still have a thriving warrior culture and one that has an unbroken legacy that will not be taken away by society, whether implied by "norms" or enforced by law.

Swiss psychoanalyst Carl Jung believed one avenue of expression for the individuation of mythos was through archetypal templating. He felt that man applied individually interpreted archetypal templates in the form of images or motifs that were conscious representations of ancient patterns. The ancient pattern of *villains and heroes* is apparent in the many representations we see in modern society. If you look at them objectively, you can see that while individual and cultural interpretations will vary--*one tribe's good guy is the next tribe's bad guy*--the symbolism and archetypal patterns are essentially the same, as are the results on the human psyche. Next, we will examine a few examples that may even sound familiar to you.

2:2. Growing up Gangster: The Ex Con

Growing up in that criminal and poverty-stricken counterculture, I was treated to the archetypes of the gangsters, mobsters and, one of the most powerful, the hardened ex-con. These archetypes and the mythology around them were so powerful that I fell victim to their influence at a very young age.

Let's look at the ex-con first. That "killer" who gets out after so many years in the hardest place on earth (in our minds) and hits the block with what seems like superpowers. He's jacked as fuck and everyone fears him. Of course, not *everyone* fears him, but they know that he is dangerous nonetheless. He symbolizes the hardening a man can achieve after being thoroughly tested and then battle-hardened, having endured one of the toughest things a man can do--prison time with the worst of the worst--and he has emerged stronger, tougher and bigger than ever.

It's hard to imagine the psyche of young males who lack proper male guidance in their lives and how susceptible they are to that negative image of raw power if you haven't lived it yourself. Having spent most of my childhood without a father or a traditional family, I can attest to the influence these strong male types have. No matter how negative, they represent power in a world that doesn't offer much else to impoverished young people. Power that they want. Women want you, and men both fear you and want to be like you.

And the *violence*. Oh yes. In poverty and the "lower class," there is often no available power other than violence. You don't have any money to sue anyone or hire an attorney if someone attacks you. There's no status protection by coming from a "good" family or a "nice" neighborhood. All you have is violence to assert your ownership over yourself, over your own life and, if need be, over another person.

The jacked, hardened ex-con personifies that violence. No one is taking shit from that guy. He gets what he wants, and he keeps what he gets. It's powerful imagery to a young mind that has grown up in a world that glorifies violence as a legitimate means to power and authority, a world that has offered that young mind no introduction to any other *tangible* means of self-empowerment or self-preservation.

A very interesting thing about prison warrior culture is that it is also saturated with ancient warrior mythos. Like the Spartans for the military and law enforcement, the convicts also call upon ancient and ancestral imagery for power. The Caucasians grasp the Viking warrior's image, or for the more extreme, the Nazi war machine. The blacks adopt and learn about the brave Zulu warriors and aspire to live up to that mythos. Hispanics look to the Aztecs, Mayans or other primitive South or Central American warrior cultures of the past.

They adopt and meld these into the personifications of the modern archetypes of the hardened convict and the gangster, a Jungian interpretation of ancient motifs. They have their images, symbols and alphabets tattooed onto their skin. I would much rather fight some 24-year-old kid who has never been to prison vs. a 24-year-old who has done five years and believes he is fighting to honor himself and his warrior ancestral pride. I say that having fought both and also having been one of them.

It's amusing to me today to see the vast commercialization of Viking imagery in particular. I mean, it is EVERYWHERE. Gyms and strength training programs are "Norse" this and "Viking" that. Tactical and fitness clothing companies have come up with every possible Viking image the human mind is capable of creating to sell on t-shirts, with some quotes about "ultimate strength until valiant death" or "no surrender, no quitting" or *whatever.* The reason I am amused personally is because way back in 1994-1999, before Crossfit and tactical clothing companies, and when the Vikings were only found in historical books, comic books, or a "mythology" class, I was wearing a Mjolnir hammer and getting runes tattooed on my body. Back then, in the context of prison life, it *meant* something to us.

Prison is a closed society, both culturally segregated and extremely violent, and inside that world, ancestral warrior imagery was a powerful symbolism to use. The young Hispanic man, barely grown, imagines the power of his Aztec ancestors, who valiantly fought against armies much more well equipped and greater in numbers and who were, for a great time, successful in beating them.

Or the young white kid imagines, as he puts on his hammer, that if his ancestors could sail across the ocean on an open ship, row that last 5 miles to shore, kick everyone's ass and take their shit, then load up and sail back home, well, surely he could wake up and face another day in prison. And if he had to fight, no fight would be as hard as the ones those great ancient warriors were victorious in. Ancient warriors whose blood runs through his very veins.

It does not matter if he is *actually* descended from them. In spirit, he is, and that is enough to invoke all of the power of the myth into his life, shoring up his orientation and making him even more dangerous to his enemies *because it is backed up with real experience in a real warrior culture.*

When your gym owner or tactical instructor gets runes tatted on him, it's cool and makes other dudes who have never done shit maybe want to be like him. When I got the word "warrior" in runes tatted on my chest in prison around 1996 or so, it was after I had experienced a particularly violent event. It was earned in blood. So, there is a definite difference in the power of symbolism and who is employing it, and what they are employing it for. The difference is in exposure to real experience vs. them imagining the action they would take if the experience ever happened. So, the gym bros in Sunnyville, USA, can't rely on the same shoring up of the orientation to be *reliable* under force pressure. We keep

53

coming back to the difference made deep at the roots of one's orientation when their experience is real, real experience vs. imagined.

And trust me, I'm not bragging (as I was so oft accused of after my first book). I would be remiss to brag about such a tragic life. I'm just speaking of historical events about my life and how it relates directly to the subject at hand, and further illustrating my points by first-hand account.

The ex-con has accumulated a very complex and vast set of experiences and paradigm shifts that have shaped his orientation in ways beyond most people's comprehension. It is essential to consider these facts deeply. There are excellent reasons that he has taken his place among the most powerful archetypes in the minds of young men in every place where poverty and violence run rampant.

2:3. The Gangster and the Mobster

The gangster is another archetype with massive power. Tony Montana, the main character in the iconic movie *Scarface*, became the shining archetypal symbol of many a young street thug wanting to be in the drug game and accumulate that wealth and power. To have the cars, the houses, the women. To have soldiers just fuck people up for you. It is a modern-day mythos that persists to this day. I can't tell you how many drug houses I walked into as a kid and saw Tony on the wall in some painting or poster, but it was more than a few, and I am certain that some of you reading this probably had that poster, too.

The mobster archetype is very much the same, but often with a different set of mythos and culture that is more "family" oriented and often just classier, maybe even a little more low-key. In the end, the imagery, the symbolism and the archetypes have the same effects on the minds of those who want to personify the stories, the legends and the myths.

Growing up in Youngstown through the '80s, the mob was just being dethroned after decades of running things. I grew up hearing the stories of these mobsters and seeing their big shiny cars rolling around town. Youngstown was a well-known mob city and, for a few decades, was the car bomb capital. One of my uncles, Roscoe, worked for some of these guys. He got me one of my first jobs with them. A big Italian guy owned a bar and a sub shop in the same building. He paid me to hang out and sweep floors and occasionally drive things here and there when I was a teenager.

This guy always had at least 3 to 4 young guys with him, sporty-looking guys who were clearly his bodyguards. I am certain I heard people get audibly "tuned up" in the backroom from time to time. Even when they weren't kicking your ass, they had these "techniques" they would use on people, like if you were talking to the big guy, one of the younger guys would come over and start massaging your shoulders, saying things like, "Relax my friend! Everything's going great. Just relax and enjoy the conversation." I can't even describe how fucking intimidating that shit was, especially to a 16-year-old kid.

I would hear them talking about all this old gangster business, who had who killed, why guys' businesses failed and, a popular one, who was banging who's wife. To hear them tell it, sometimes it sounded like more busts, raids and murders happened over adulterous affairs than actual business. But these guys had a few key things: power, money, and women. Now take a guess what three things will ignite desire in the mind of the young, impoverished male. I think you know the answer to that.

An old mobster saved my ass once when I first got locked up. I was brand new, and it was my first week at a real prison, having been transported from the county jail to a "receiving prison," which is the place you go to while they sort out which parent institution you will be shipped to serve out your sentence at. As you can imagine, receiving was a rough place because there was no separation of different security levels. You were locked up with everyone going to prison: killers, rapists, gangbangers, maniacs...everyone.

Despite my upbringing, I was still a dumbass teenage kid, and I got into some trouble the first week. I allowed a few guys, who I did not know, to talk me into a "friendly" card game of spades. I was partnered up with a pretty hardcore-looking inmate who looked like this wasn't his first or second trip through the system. My partner and I lost and, while I thought we were just passing the time, apparently, there was some type of bet on the game. As I would learn, gambling is one of the fastest ways to get fucked up in prison. So my partner was apparently pissed at me and was planning to fuck me up.

I was sort of oblivious to this until this big, loud, hairy-chested Italian guy comes over and says, "Hey kid, come walk with me." Back in the 90's prisons were overflowing, and they probably had a few hundred of us shoved in a big gymnasium with bunk beds just lined up in rows. Walking the outside perimeter of the gym was the only exercise you could get, and it also gave you a 360-degree view of everyone and everything in the room.

Now, you have to understand this guy was the real deal. He was a high-ranking law enforcement officer in a small-town department. It was common for corrupt and connected people to run all public offices and local government back then. His office was wiretapped, and he was set up for a corruption case and convicted. So, on the one hand, he's an ex-cop in prison, and he has to assume he's going to be targeted. On the other hand, he's a connected guy with a last name that was very well known in crime families nationally and internationally. Either way, he had a hell of a reputation to live up to.

So, I'm walking around with this big Italian, and he's sending a message to the whole fucking room. He is talking very loudly. He keeps saying in his stereotypical Italian *Goodfellas* accent, *"These motherfuckers don't know what balls are! I got the biggest fucking balls in this whole goddamn place! I'll show these motherfuckers how big my fuckin balls are! Anybody wants to fuck with you; they're gonna be fuckin with me! And I got big fuckin balls to be fuckin with me. I don't give a fuck who they are!"*

It took me a few minutes to realize this guy was protecting me. He saw some shit about to go down that I wasn't even fully aware of, and he stepped in and put me under his protection. And he never wanted a thing from me. He kept those guys off me until we all got separated into cell blocks and finally put in cells as they were opening up. He even came to talk to my family during a visitation in the visiting room and introduced me to his beautiful wife and mother. He said, pointing to his family, "Tell em, I didn't let nobody fuck with you in there did I?" He wanted them to know he helped me out.

Now, I could tell that guy was a real *motherfucker*. I have no doubt he had really fucked some people over before. But for me, he was a great guy. I never saw him again after that, and I certainly hope things turned out good for him. He saved my ass, and I will always be grateful for that because he didn't have to, and he didn't get anything out of it. I have no idea why he did it; I never even had a chance to ask him. I was a dumbass teenage kid getting in over my head, and he fucking pulled me back up on my feet.

He was the mob guy, the loud gangster with "the biggest fucking balls" there. So the mythos weren't just some stories; they were real to us. These guys really existed, the gangsters, the mobsters, the convicts, and killers; we knew them well.

The more hardcore mythos, especially the street soldier, gangster and ex-con archetypes, reached a critical momentum back in the '90s with gangster rap. I personally put Tupac at the top of the game (in my mind, he is the all-time king of real gangster rap). These guys, back then, rapped about life on the streets, about going to prison and shooting people and getting shot. And guess what?

In their real lives, these guys went to prison, shot people, and got shot. The two disputed kings of rap of that time, Tupac and Biggie Smalls, were both shot to death (each accused of the other's death in one way or another). I was also locked up at the same time Pac did his time in prison. I was still in when his new post-prison album dropped, and I heard every word every day in there, blasting from boomboxes all over the compound. That mindset was prevalent at that time, especially in prison.

Although I wasn't a fan back then, it was quite literally the soundtrack for daily life in prison and in the lives of those who ended up there. If you listen to Tupac Shakur and a few others from that era, they absolutely captured this spirit in such a dramatic way because these were guys who lived these mythos and perpetuated them. They grew up with these conditions that I described earlier, the lack of positive guidance and the allure of the negative role models, and they embodied the archetypal spirit gangster/convict and morphed themselves into becoming it:

"Back in elementary, I thrived on misery. Left me alone I grew up amongst a dyin' breed. Inside my mind couldn't find a place to rest . Until I got that Thug Life tatted on my chest" (So Many Tears, Tupac Shakur)

Tupac poetically describes this condition and demonstrates that he understood, at a very deep level, that he was a product of that environment and of that process of wanting to be among that warrior culture. Of course, later in his life, Tupac began to preach about this condition directly and speak out about the problem and how it is perpetuated in the cycle of life in the ghettos of the U.S.

Nowadays, I can genuinely appreciate Pac's music as it has become quite nostalgic for me, and in no other music can I find relatable lyrics and feelings that remind me that we were not alone in having grown up without positive male role models, with domestic abuse, drug abuse and alcoholism, family and friends dying and being murdered, violence and prison...in short, songs about life as I remember it to be from my childhood and young adulthood.

That particular period of rap also exhibited that age-old adage of *Momento Mori*, to remember you will die:

"My every move is a calculated step, to bring me closer, to embrace an early death, now there's nothin" left" (So Many Tears, Tupac Shakur).

It's easy to overlook the very deep and powerful implications of such statements, especially if you overestimate your own position as a "good guy" and look down on these types of archetypes, such as "thug life" soldiers, making the grave mistake of underestimating your opponents.

But do so at your own peril. While mainstream rap has now settled down to being dominated by face-tattooed mumble rappers that largely don't have real violence backgrounds, the street soldier mythos still does very much exist. The archetype is powerful enough to experience a resurgence, especially if an economic catalyst comes along, such as a crash or another drug explosion like the crack game of the late '80s and early '90s.

There are many warriors out there on the streets that are comfortable with the thought of their own death, *as long as they die like a "soldier."* Just look to the murder rates of some cities, and more specifically certain neighborhoods in those cities. There is *a lot* of cold-blooded killing going on out there…

When you are dealing with a criminal fighter, you may be dealing with someone who has a dream, who has strong symbols and mythology, with powerful archetypes that would crush enemies like you in their stories. Those mythos and visions may be different than yours in context, **but in general content and in the result they have on the mind, they are the same as the stories you tell yourself.**

The more we remember that we are not different from one another, the more level the field becomes between us and them. As much as many of you pull on the mythos of the ancient warrior, like the aforementioned Spartan, you also have your modern cultural heroes: Audie Murphy, Chesty Puller, the SAS guy who single-handedly stormed the hotel in Kenya in January 2019 to fight several terrorists and save hundreds of people, the countless nameless images of special operations guys "doing work" against the bad guys, the lists go on and on. This is no different than Tony Montana, the mobster, the gangster, the drug dealer kingpin, and even the stone-cold killer, at least as far as your opponent is concerned. The archetypes serve the same purpose.

These inspirational stories make up a huge influence on your orientation and the decisions you will make when faced with the type of pressures that these mythos are designed to address. Be careful how you choose your own, and do not make the mistake of downplaying the archetypes of your enemies.

2:4. The Righteous Hero

For most people, the dark or negative side of the personality remains unconscious. The hero, on the contrary, must realize that the shadow exists and that he can draw strength from it. -Carl Jung

Many self-defense instructors, including professional trainers in military and law enforcement, like to teach that the dangerous criminal or enemy fighter is somehow *different* from you. Like they are dangerous and evil, which somehow makes them almost a completely different species. Some misguided mythos have been created for this, making the bad guys wolves and the good guys sheepdogs. But this thinking is flawed in many ways.

The "bad guys" are humans, just like you. They have fears, insecurities, attachments, values, experience, mythos and stories, archetypes and heroes. They have an orientation and a process for analysis and synthesis. They can have acute clarity or be susceptible to incestuous amplification. They have good days and bad days. The sooner one realizes that the enemy is just like oneself, the sooner one masters that enemy and levels that battlefield.

Stories matter greatly. They guide our mythology and create the inspiration or fear-mongering needed for us to be sufficiently compelled to perform and feel in particular ways. Religions promise utopia for good behavior and unending torment for bad. We tell our children of a bogey man that steals children and hurts them to keep them from talking to strangers. Our society is full of such stories that inspire and guide our decision-making.

But those telling the stories that bad guys are "not like you!" are pushing a narrative of the ferocious beast in the woods that will devour you with mindless brutality while ignoring the *victim* story embedded inside it.

Yes, you want to think that the audience of civilians and law enforcement are courageous and strong enough to see themselves as some sort of hero that victoriously slays beasts. Still, in reality, most average people in our modern-day society are a far cry from seeing themselves as raging heroes.

The people packing most training classes and police academies are inexperienced and lack the confidence necessary to feel victorious when faced with the horrible, pure evil that is continually described to them. Telling them about the evil, vicious beast is fear-mongering, and while that is an effective tool to create emotion and even some action, it is not a sound method for building a strong orientation for doing battle with these bad people.

What you end up with is someone who views the bad guy as this other type of creature far more capable of violence and darkness than they could ever be. They lack the experience and courage to know that they could be victorious if faced with such efficient evil. They are victims, weaker and more civilized in a world with wild beasts roaming about, incapable of making the decisions of violence and terror that these bad people are capable of making. Oh, but make those decisions; you must! To be your own hero, you must master the dark side of life--and, most importantly, of yourself--before you are able to meet the bad guy head-on in battle. As Carl Jung states, man *"must realize that the shadow exists and that he can draw strength from it."* When advising professionals and armed citizens about the decision to use lethal force on another human, it is often taught that a person must premeditatively find that ability inside of themself to consciously take another person's life from them.

This is a huge deal for most people. Many are just not sure if they can even decide at all. It requires confronting that darkside of the human mind and coming to some terms, internally, with the act of ending another's life. Without it, sure, you may panic and pull a gun and successfully defend yourself in a fit of fear and adrenaline, but the aftermath can be horrific psychologically because you were not fully prepared to make those decisions; therefore, you may now struggle with it afterward. Your orientation was not prepared for the load of that event, and you will suffer what is known as *moral injury*, the root of one of the worst types of PTSD out there. This happens to civilians, cops and soldiers alike.

It can be devastating and often is for many people. (We're not even talking about the mistakes and legal aftermath nightmare that can be created for someone who is acting out of panic instead of acting on training and planning.)

This is the very same capability that we are talking about in the bad guy. They can murder and rape and will often be ok with it afterward. What we call a "conscience" is merely a social construct based on the norms of our society, and when someone does not agree with those norms, they appear to us not to have a "conscience." They will always go further than you or the hero of your story. But the hero must at least harness a significant portion of that darkness to survive that type of encounter physically and psychologically whole. It requires a different look at the norms we adhere to. A perfect example of this is the dark side hero story in Marvel's *Punisher* series.

During the second season of the popular Netflix show, Frank *The Punisher,* a vigilante hero and former special operations soldier that punishes bad people with highly illegal, terroristic beatings and murder, is psychologically devastated by being led to believe that he accidentally murdered several innocent women while in a fit of rage.

This was part of a diabolical plan to destroy the Punisher's will to fight by *"taking away what is most valuable to him, his belief that he is righteous."* Of course, Frank's equally law-breaking law enforcement friends save him by uncovering the plot and restoring Frank's belief in his righteousness, which empowers him to once again go forth and mercilessly murder bad guys because he is the *"righteous hero."*

In that scenario, even though Frank is a stone-cold killer, he was not willing to kill innocent women. He has a code, a *conscience*. The bad guys had no problem with it, nor did they have a problem identifying these vulnerable components of Frank's orientation and breaking his will by using them against him. *They successfully used his own story against him.*

Amazingly, it's the very same theme I see pushed in the defense training world, having that willingness to kill but to have a *code of honor* distinctly different than the "bad" guy. But there is a problem with this *righteousness* story for us. You can not go forth and dole out justice by mercilessly killing bad guys; it's illegal to premeditatively murder someone, no matter what the cause. However, what you must do is find that killer inside yourself to be willing to potentially end the lives of one or two bad people if you need to someday, *as a result of you effectively defending yourself or another* - and you have to be OK with it. But, you can't *render justice*. That is the difference, and that is the danger of the "righteous hero."

2:5. Justified by Law vs. Justified by Righteousness

When your mythos are based upon "righteousness," you are inherently taking on a belief system centered around your ideas of "justice." The killing of bad guys or enemy combatants becomes a justified act to you personally because you are "righteous," and they are not. The truth is that legally you can not render justice, and your orientation, your *mindset*, and all of your training must reflect this truth at the core of your mission, or you will fail to differentiate between *justified by law* and *justified by righteousness*.

Similarly, religiously based terrorists are nearly always operating off the powerful beliefs of righteous justification. They believe unequivocally that they are on the right side of justice, the good guys in the battle against evil. Those fighting against them believe the same thing, yet they most often lack the *religious* conviction, with centuries of culture, tradition and incredibly strong mythos backing that belief up.

This puts the anti-terrorist fighter at a deficit of conviction. Terrorists driven by *religious* righteousness will willingly die for their cause and often believe in great rewards in the afterlife for such sacrifice. The average soldier in a modern, western world military will not have such beliefs.

This is not much different than the street thug gang banger that believes he is fighting for survival in a world that hates him, who is invested fully in the glory of dying in battle and how he will live forever in the memory of his people, vs. the cop who is just an average person trying to do a job. There's a disparity of orientation-based conviction there.

The first task at hand is to be self-aware enough not to fall victim to righteous justification. *Your orientation can not be developed off of stories and traditions that paint a one-sided view of the world, of history and of how conflict is justified in your life.* You also must recognize the sheer power of mind and the dedication that such beliefs will give your enemy. Those with such deep convictions are not to be trifled with lightly.

2:6. Overcoming the Conviction Disparity

Many people who carry a gun, often know more about their own righteous hero story than they do about the actual laws in the State that they would be defending themselves in. This means they walk around with the belief that *no matter what,* they will be justified because they are "the good guy." (To truly understand what I am saying here, it is recommended that you go back and read the "Mission" section in my first book, *Violence of Mind.*)

What does not apply to your own real-life mission from this hero story is the ability to bend and break the rules. As a citizen, a cop, or even a soldier, you must stay within the rules and the law. If you wanted to talk about one huge difference between you and the bad guy, it is the fact that you have very specific rules and laws that you must follow. For you, there definitely are rules in a fight. For him, there are none. Therefore, our own hero stories have to have this feature built into them to be truly effective in aiding us to complete our mission.

Like our training, which must have these laws and limitations built into every drill, skill, technique and procedure, our mythos and stories that we tell ourselves must be constructed with these laws and limitations built into them as well. You can not walk around the streets of any U.S. city, envisioning yourself as a righteous good guy that can indiscriminately smoke bad guys at will, like the fictional character Frank *The Punisher.* It will get you put in prison, or worse.

I know that sounds dumb to read, but I can't tell you how many times I have heard that exact self-story being told at gun store counters and on social media. *"If he's in my house, he's DEAD!"* or *"If someone starts a robbery when I'm around, I WILL kill him and make sure he's dead!"* That and seeing the amount of Punisher logo parts sold for guns in the U.S. every day...you get the idea. That is what justification by righteousness sounds and looks like.

What is widely known as "good guy syndrome" is not rooted in reality because "righteousness" is a subjective, culturally influenced, but largely individual notion. In contrast, legal justification is governed by the laws and the perceptions of those who are interpreting those laws and applying them to judge your actions, such as a prosecutor, judge, or jurors.

This is very important to mindset and self-control because it is a core component of orientation. If you simply believe you are "righteous" and haven't properly aligned yourself with the laws, you can make several mistakes. These mistakes can include anything from going too far in the application of force and breaking the law to becoming overconfident and making a fatal mistake costing you your life. You are creating the criteria for incestuous amplification to see what you *want* to see instead of what is really there.

As with most good hero stories, there is some truth in *The Punisher*. The theme of Frank's story is that he is a trained killer, it's what he does, and the only thing that separates him from the bad guys is *who* he chooses to beat and murder. And therein lies the truth: to be truly capable of doing battle with an extremely violent, murderous enemy, you have to be just as capable and just as willing to inflict harm to them as they are to you.

Yes, you choose much more selectively who you do it to, but *it is the same act*. It is the *perceived* darkness of humankind that you must not only acknowledge but harness. Unless you want to skate through on luck and panic and deal with a harsh psychological aftermath *if* you survive the encounter at all, then you must locate, deal with, and harness this part of human existence within yourself. Your enemy certainly has, and that is worth some very deep thought. You just can not get lost in the rabbit hole of righteous justification and imagined capabilities, which leads one astray from the realities of legal justification and an accurate sense of capability.

You overcome the disparity of conviction by constructing a solid foundation in your orientation and one that results in you fully believing in yourself, your decisions and your capabilities with realistic accuracy. Your trained responses and skills, your mythos and archetypes, and your attitudes are all based upon legally defensible adherence to the laws around you. Your confidence is true and earned through hundreds or thousands of hours of practice and pressure testing in non-compliant environments. Your cultural beliefs are strong, and your conscience is cleared of any wrongdoing since your actions are motivated by not only what you sense is "right" but also limited to what is legally justified.

You have eliminated questions that could come up and cause hesitation in the heat of the moment. You know who you are, why you are there, what you are capable of and allowed to do, and you are confident in all of it 100%. True conviction and dedication emerge from such a foundation.

2:7. The "Just a Guy" Guy

There's one more story we should look at here. He's the guy who just read this about the others, the gangsters and the Spartans, and thought, "That's dumb; I don't need that nonsense to have courage, strength and honor." He's *just a guy*.

But he tells himself a story, too. Maybe it's his muscles and his deadlift max or his tattoos and his motorcycle. Maybe it's his top-shelf bourbon and his very expensive truck. Or perhaps it's his dedication to training in shooting, strength and combatives. It could be the "real man" archetype that drives him, his cultural version of what that is: like being strong, providing for his family, standing up to all of life's challenges.

Whatever it is, he grasps it and pulls it into the center of his life to build his identity around it, to create the image of who he wants to be, or more importantly, **who he wants others to believe he is**. He projects the image he envisions through the eyes of others because that is what this is really for at that level, the perceptions of others.

And this doesn't just apply to the tough guy. It's the person who desperately wants to fit in with "successful" or "rich" people, so he or she uses clothing, cars and mannerisms (behavioral modeling) to create a persona that would appear to put them in that higher bracket. It's the person who wants to move up in the company, so they become shrewd and fiercely loyal to the corporation, the "manager today, CEO tomorrow" archetype. I've even met guys who were in business and marketing and who fashioned themselves in the image of Don Draper, the ruthless and womanizing marketing wizard and completely fictional character from the show *Mad Men*.

They tell themselves a story, and it's a story they were told by someone else. It said to them, "*This* is what is cool. *This* is what holds power, prestige. And this is how you get it, how you *take* it." So, they wanted to become that.

Some actually do become it. Some fake it until they make it. And some, *I would argue most*, just simply fake it. But make no mistake, there's no human out there operating at normal cognitive and social levels that is not telling themselves a story about who they are and how they fit into the world around them. And when you correctly decipher what that story is, you gain access to the keys that switch their emotions and decision-making factors on and off.

2:8. Stories Can and *Do* Come True.

Just because an individual has not self-actualized in their chosen story yet does not mean that they never will. It could be you that they use to catapult themselves up into the manifestation of these visions of themselves. A violent or initiation-type event involving you may be the event that makes their bones and brings them to the height of their story, so underestimating someone because they haven't done it *yet* is a mistake.

It reminds me of when I was trapped against my will by a crazy guy. We'll call him "Dutch." I was about 14 or 15, and Dutch was probably in his early 30's maybe. We were at the house of a mutual acquaintance drinking and smoking, and Dutch suddenly took a serious dislike towards me. This is a common occurrence in the slums and drug houses, situations and people can turn violent with very little warning or provocation.

He attacked me in a fit of rage, threw me into a back room, and did not let me out of the room. He would come in and mildly torture me by bending my wrists backward or twisting my shoulder joint until it burned, all the while screaming at me with his face red with rage and spit spattering out of his mouth. He was obviously high and drunk and had a very serious anger problem. I was definitely worried, but I was also still talking shit the whole time, telling him, *"you have no idea who my family is; your fucking ass is dead if you hurt me!"*

He replied, *"I have a trunk full of explosives in my car. I'll fucking blow your mom's house up and kill your whole family motherfucker!"*

It's interesting to note that the "friends" I thought I had there refused to get involved or help me. Dutch was, in fact, a very large and scary guy. I could tell that he wasn't ready to kill me, and although I didn't really know him or know much about him, I chose not to provoke a physical fight. He had his temper tantrum, and eventually, everyone was like, *"Hey, let him go, Dutch. He's not doing anything."* He let me come out, and then we parted ways. I never hung around him again.

What's interesting is that at that time, while Dutch was known for being a hell of a brawler, he wasn't yet the killer that he obviously believed himself to be. At least he had not acted on it. But that day did come, and just a year or two after our confrontation.

He got into a fight with another guy at one of our local dive bars. Dutch stabbed the guy to death in the men's toilet of the bar. That guy misjudged him, and he died on the piss-soaked floor of a dive bar on the edge of the slums. In one of the rarest moments of court history, Dutch actually got acquitted for the murder. A big factor for that conclusion was that only two men were present for the fight, and one of them was dead, so the court only heard Dutch's side.

I remember being in the local housing projects maybe six months to a year after his acquittal and seeing Dutch, from a distance, jump on the hood of his ex-girlfriend's car and kick her windshield in with his cowboy boot while she was trying to leave him. Rather than changing his ways on the heels of almost doing life in prison, he was now the killer he sought to be, and he wasn't showing any signs of slowing down.

I have no idea what happened to Dutch after that. I'd place hard bets that it most likely hasn't ended well for him in the 30 years that's passed since then. The takeaway here is that two very violent guys crossed paths--guys who both went on to stab people multiple times--and that day could have easily been *the* event for either one of us. One or two years later, Dutch stabbed a man to death in a bar, and three or four years later, I stabbed a man 23 times in a house. That day was a close call, but we both went on to have our events later with other opponents.

How many close calls have you had? How many times have you underestimated someone because of your disbelief that murderous violence would happen to you, or because when someone says, *"I'll fucking kill you!"* you never take it seriously because it rarely actually happens? Pay attention to that story; just because it isn't real yet doesn't mean that it never will be. An *initiation* may certainly happen.

2:9. The Initiation

Men seek out war, or prison, or gangland warfare, because they want to experience the genuine trials of the hero, to endure the initiation of pain to be reborn a hardened man. Young men often feel called to establish themselves in this way. This has been a theme throughout all of mankind's recorded thoughts.

Nothing is as powerful to cement a story into the mind of the believer as having endured an initiation, something that tested the individual in ways relevant to the story and optimally was dangerous and could have resulted in death. The enduring of war, or prison, or some other extreme hardship where death is not only possible but very often imminent, is like a trip through a hell of sorts where one is tested, tortured and then hardened. It is essentially the "hero's journey." Even Adolf Hitler, one of the most heinous villains in human history, knew this when he said that *"war is to a man what childbirth is to a woman."* Initiation is not a secret. It is sought out instinctually by people of all cultures, regardless of notions of good or bad.

You may be thinking, "This is bullshit; who would think such things?" I can assure you that I, myself, thought such things. As did many other men I have spoken with who have gone through similar ordeals in life. I remember a very telling and pivotal time when I was locked up as a juvenile. I was in the juvenile jail, and although I can't remember for what, I can assure you it was related to fighting.

A traveling "ministry" came in to talk sense into us kids, an endeavor that rarely reached its goal. The "preachers" were tattooed ex-cons who had "found Jesus" and wanted to share the good news that we didn't have to experience this horrible life that was being laid out in front of most of us. But what they failed to understand is that, whether they had "found Jesus" or not, they still represented hardened men that had experienced and survived some of the most badass trials and tribulations a young man can face. So, to us, their stories about their criminal life and what led up to them getting locked up were way more interesting to us than how Jesus could make us feel good inside.

I distinctly remember one guy talking about being a coke dealer, how he had Mercedes-Benz cars and money and girls, and how none of that mattered when he went to jail.

All we heard was Mercedes, money, girls and *tough guy* shit. In a very pivotal moment, as they were describing the horrors of prison--the violence, the rapes, the treatment by the guards--one of the preachers asked the question, "Who in this room thinks they are going to prison?" One solitary 14-year-old kid raised his hand. That kid was me. I wanted to go to this place they were describing as so terrible. I wanted to prove, to the world and to myself, that I could take that shit. No fucking problem. I got this. I have what it takes to do this. I have what it takes to become one of the hardest men that ever lived.

Little did I know what a hell that would actually be, many years later, after all of the glory is gone and you are left only with the scars, injuries and the tattered parts of your life that you managed to salvage. How even 20 years later, you'll be denied jobs or places to live because of it. Nope, no one talked about that part of it. But back then, it seemed totally reasonable. This is a sad story and one that I hate telling. I hate admitting that I was a 14-year-old kid that glorified the thought of going to prison because I wanted to be a tough guy and because I looked up to my hard-ass uncles, who all went to prison. I am able to tell it because I will not take the blame as a 14-year-old kid for having those thoughts.

Most of the men in my family had been to prison, either State or federal. I admired their confidence. They were all strong, tough, successful with women, and commanded respect from everyone around them. I wanted that. I wanted that *zero fucks* attitude. That role model was powerful, especially when everyone in the family, including the women, would just praise how tough and violent the men were.

I would listen closely to the stories they would tell about the time Uncle Tom knocked out the guy in the snow, or when he fought five guys in a restaurant parking lot and won, or when Uncle Kenny caught the guy sleeping with his wife and shot him in the backyard. The stories were endless, and they came with great praise and enthusiasm.

And they weren't just stories! These experiences were still happening up through my teenage years. I remember one time in particular when I got a first-hand lesson about intimidation, door breaching and giving zero fucks from my Uncle Roscoe. Some guys were giving me trouble down in the projects (low-income housing apartment complex one street over from our house). They had jumped me, and 5 or 6 of them had given me a pretty good beating. I was maybe 13 or 14 at the time, and I went and told Roscoe what was going on.

Now, Roscoe was a scary dude. He was probably in his 40's at the time and had done time in prison, including a stretch in El Paso for armed robbery, in one of the toughest prisons in the country. He had also survived a nasty drunk car wreck where he had ripped a Mercury Comet completely in half and was thrown 25 yards into a field with his skull split from front to back, leaving this crazy-ass scar running from his eye socket back through his forehead to the back of his head. He walked on a cane, but that didn't detract from his absolute fucking scariness. There was no doubt he was a "stick-up guy" from way back. Sometimes he was meaner than shit, even to me, but I loved him. He was one of the main male role models in my childhood.

Upon hearing about the big guys and adults who were giving me trouble, he said, *"Come on, let's go handle this fucking shit."* We loaded up in the car and drove straight to the apartment the dudes all hung out in. We walked right up to the apartment and listened. There were quite a few voices inside, which is apparently what Roscoe wanted to hear. He reached up and softly checked the doorknob. It was unlocked. He very, very slowly turned the knob and nudged the door until the latch bolt was just clear of the hole, leaving the door ready to swing open.

This told him that the deadbolt was also unlocked and prepped the door for breach. In one swift motion and incredibly fast for a guy on a fucking cane, my uncle kicked open the door and moved right into the center of the room. He dominated that room in one second. It was *his*. The shocked look on the 7 or 8 faces sitting around stoned and caught off guard was amazing. I learned some very valuable things that day about surprise and people's reactions to being overwhelmed when they are not expecting it.

Roscoe then gave the most gangster warning I've heard to this day, *"I heard you punk motherfuckers are fucking with my nephew. You motherfuckers better ask somebody about me. I'm Roscoe motherfuckers; I will kill every one of you bitch motherfuckers in this room. Go ahead, and fucking try me, I ain't got nothing to lose, and I don't give a fuck about this life or this world at all. I ain't afraid to die, and I sure as fuck won't think twice about killing every one of you."*

This dude was standing in the middle of a room full of teen and young adult males from the *'hood*. Them, young and strong and him, busted up and older, and he was totally dominating them. Guys that I had seen act tough and mean now in front of my very eyes were scared, legitimately scared. I have no idea what Roscoe would have done had he been challenged, but I knew for sure he wasn't worried about it. He breached that door and took that room, and this was the absolute definition of giving zero fucks.

You could tell he had done this and worse many times. He was confident, like no one else in the room. He knew how they were going to act before they knew it. That day he was the apex predator in that room. I wanted that power. I wanted that level of recognition. I now knew exactly what it was like, participating in taking that room from these fucks who had threatened and beat me and taking that power from them. That was intoxicating. My fate was sealed. I was officially in training.

So, yes, when that day came later on, and I was sitting in that room in juvenile jail, I raised my hand, and I meant it. I was ready to go, and I would do well. If anyone in that room had what it takes to make it, it was me. The event with Roscoe and the breaking and entering was only one of *many* that happened to prepare me for that. The events of my adolescence grew more violent and more tragic until there was a great crescendo ending with me defending myself against a drunk, high attacker with multiple friends and eventually going to prison, as predicted.

In retrospect, I sorely wish that someone would have guided me into the military, as that would have been a much better trial for the quality of my life. Being a felon is a stigma that lasts forever, long after the effects of the small power and street glory have faded. I did try, but Clinton's military was super-picky and told me "no" several times because I would have been a G.E.D. entrant, and they only wanted "the best applicants." They had no idea what the best was made of, I'm sure. So, prison, it was.

The reason I am sharing this story with you is that, after all, we are here to answer the question, *"How does one build the proper mindset for extreme violence?"* The answer is that it is necessary to develop your *orientation* at a very deep level. So, there was just one example of how that happened for me. The training started very early and was deeply refined through years of repetitive exposure to violence and violent behaviors. That is the easy part to understand, and you can try to mimic that with your training classes and mindset visualization and self-talk.

What you can not emulate are the rites of passage, the initiations, and the years of programming that come before and after them to burn the lessons in. You can not simulate living life and doing battle with absolutely no rules. Truly living with *zero fucks given* during any operation or daily contact with other people is something that few experience and virtually no one experiences outside of the criminal realm. Unless you are a criminal, you will never know what that feels like, nor will your mindset ever be able to truly grasp that condition.

For some men, it is the allure of war. For others, it is the path of the gangster or the hardass that emerges through prison or street warfare. Just be sure to understand that the enemy you may face someday very likely has some rite of passage behind him and has *proven* to himself and the world that he has what it takes to survive and dominate. This is a powerful component to a strong mythos because the warrior is not simply a believer; he is a participant, a survivor, a *veteran* of the story. His belief is stronger than the uninitiated could ever understand because **the mythos is backed up by successful experience** and that real experience is irreplaceable in a world fraught with death and uncertainty.

This is why try as they might; some people just truly can not be the kind of warrior their personal mythos would tell them they are. If you have lived a decent life and escaped the trappings of war and violent crime, you missed the bus to Hardassville, and you are lucky for the most part. Sure, you can come close with years of going hard in your training and grueling transformations of yourself; that DOES count for a lot. But confidence from experience, especially that born of a big death-defying act like surviving prison, military war, or gang warfare, gives you something that can not be attained by any other means. It brings the mythos to life and makes the believer one with the heroes of his stories.

Lucky you, having skipped that experience, you will also skip the post-traumatic stress conditions, the nightmares, the difficulty in coping with and co-existing with the uninitiated civilian population. You also get to skip the stigma of being a felon in a world that is able to legally discriminate against you in every way imaginable or of being a combat vet that is suddenly isolated because he isn't understood by those he was once the closest to in life.

The takeaways? Know your limitations, and do not underestimate your enemy's confidence via his experience. Our mythos are powerful, but there must be initiations and rites of passage that give that story the real element of power. Experience is what makes your mythos real. Think of it this way, if you know someone who has never been a cop or stepped inside of a prison or been in the military or even a regular member of a gym. Yet, they portray a "warrior" image and obviously subscribe to the mythos, then you KNOW they are full of shit. This is easy.

What is not so easy is knowing when you *yourself* are full of shit. Convincing yourself that you are among "the initiated" because you took some classes, ran a Spartan race, or did the Murph for the last three years, or because you have taken jiu-jitsu for eight years and can shoot really well is a mistake. The cool gear, the cool truck, the belt, the patches...it all screams *badass*. You are creating an image of the Instagram-friendly warrior, but maybe not so much real life. Real-life is the guy next to you at the red light in the shitty old school Buick Regal with faded paint that has been gang banging since he was 11, has been in 3 drive-bys, four gunfights and probably 100 fistfights, and who **sees his future performance through the lens of successful past performance**. His Glock is near his lap with a drum mag in it. If he decides to blast you, he will act with conviction, malice and confidence. That is the result of a true initiation process. And that is the difference you must learn, understand and then work to emulate as closely as possible.

Some may think that sounds overly dramatic or unrealistic, but we see this in video examples with officers making traffic stops all the time. The officer goes from lax to being surprised when a gun is thrown in his or her face and they are being shot at before they even know what's happening. This is a mindset problem, not a skill-set problem. I am sure all of those officers passed their weapons qualification (though that does not equal skill assurance).

I am also sure that some of those officers are actually fast and accurate with their pistols. But as I have said many times on many platforms, skills are utterly useless when you can't clearly make the decision to use them in time. Sometimes they lose because the enemy's ambush is just that good. Sometimes they lose because they are not taking the job and its risks seriously enough. But at the core of it, the initiated always take the risks of the job seriously because they have met death and defied it before. It's literally one of the built-in purposes of initiations.

2:10. Solving the Initiation Problem

So how do we then solve this mindset problem of being deficient of actual experience or death-defying survivorship? Training and simulation are only partial solutions. You must find a way to recreate the psychological effect that such initiations have as closely as possible. The initiation is only a component, an *add-on*, of orientation. Some people do not have it as part of their orientation. It happens separately from the rest of your experiences; it stands out.

As I talked about in the previous section, some people seek it out. I sought it out, however misguided, through prison. Others look for their own crucible in the military or in a career in law enforcement in a dangerous city. Young men often seem to be born with this innate need to test and prove themselves; it is part of the male psyche (although society is trying to beat that out of us today).

One place we can look to see this initiation phenomenon manifest itself in very negative ways is in the inner-city youths, especially those who grow up without fathers or positive male role models. I'll remind you here, I was one of those kids, so I'm not talking from some observation point in an ivory tower. It happened to me, and I've already explained that process. But let's look at the gang problem in particular. Young boys who grow up impoverished and lacking guidance often end up feeling like aggression and materialism are the only ways to prove their worth and establish their place in the dominance hierarchy that we all live within (and like it or not, you *do* live within it).

Those neighborhoods are often very rough and violent, and the homes within them are riddled with alcoholism, drug addiction, violence and apathy, just as my childhood home was. The outside world, the suburbs, schools, privileged kids, the police and basically everyone else views these boys as trouble. They are treated differently outside of their neighborhoods; if they walk through a nicer neighborhood, the eyes are on them, the police are called, and they are usually questioned about why they are even there.

Having been one of those kids who got harassed even when I wasn't doing anything wrong, today I don't hold it against society and neighborhoods who are vigilant and want to maintain their security and peace by keeping the riff-raff out. It's just the way it is, and now that I am a father in my 40's I have the exact same proclivities when I am scanning my own neighborhood. However, it doesn't change the experience for the young boys who are unwelcomed in most places outside of their shitty ghetto world.

Overall, growing up in one of these violent, oppressive and neglectful places is a certain way to raise rogue warriors. It is a very negative experience, and it begins to build a violent orientation towards the world and other human beings in a very deep, dark way. Young boys are formed psychologically within this paradigm, and they lack the guidance of mature men to show them what is important in life and how to control and direct that young male energy.

They often look at women as objects of desire and utility and use aggression and money (materialism) to be successful at mating (l won't get into how the young women are conditioned to respond to this treatment here because that is a topic worthy of a better perspective than my own). Suffice it to say that a criminally violent orientation is built, layer upon layer, year after year, negative experience upon negative experience. It is then reinforced with its own culture, its own rules of conduct, its own mythos and heroes, and even its own music. The ultimate reinforcement of it comes in the form of initiations that forge the hero from the fire.

You can not expect to emulate that no more than you could match the conviction of a zealot or religious terrorist. But you can build an orientation that is also clear and free from the clutter and contamination of false beliefs, biases and outright lies that will lead to mistakes in decision making. While such convictions make that fighter fierce and hard to face, it will also make them run headlong into their own certain death. With clarity, preparation, training and a clean orientation, you can become the deliverer of that death, all within the legal justification of the laws and policies under which you are judged.

There are three major components to a readiness mindset for deadly force 1) acknowledging the existence of extreme violence and the chance we may be exposed to it; 2) issuing deadly force against another human being and; 3) dealing with the aftermath of participating in that level of violence. Let's look at each of them one by one.

2:11. Facing the Reality of Violence

"The impact of this horror on a sensitive consciousness is terrific-- this monster which is life. Life is a horrendous presence, and you wouldn't be here if it weren't for that. The first function of a mythological order has been to reconcile consciousness to this fact."
-Joseph Campbell

On Friday, March 15, 2019, at least one gunman attacked mosques in New Zealand and systematically exterminated people for about 30 minutes. Fifty people were killed, and 50 people were wounded. Among the dead and wounded were men, women, children, and the elderly. The shooter live-streamed the attack with a POV camera that gave the viewer a first-person shooter perspective of the killing very clearly. The videos were uploaded to several places on the internet and viewed millions of times before authorities could begin taking them down.

Watching the reactions of people on social media to the New Zealand mosque shooting videos confirmed what I already knew about average people, including people in the self-defense and gun training communities. Many people just do not have what it takes to deal with hardcore violence, where life is devalued to worthlessness. Most of the people I interacted with on social media who were also heavily involved in violence training were not able to watch the videos at all. They just couldn't do it. They could not watch the uncensored, first-person video of men, women, children, and elderly being gunned down with a rifle at room distance.

To develop the orientation needed to deal with it efficiently enough to stay focused on work, people would have to give up a significant part of their worldview, their current orientation. People do not want to acknowledge or actively believe they live in a dangerous world where someone would put their children down like dogs with an anchor shot to the skull right in front of them. They don't want to think like that because they would feel unsafe every second of every day. I know this because I feel the presence of that constant awareness in the background of my own mind.

Why would I feel the pressure of constant threat? The layers are many. I once had a cellmate who killed five prostitutes, each with repeated blows from a claw hammer. He calmly told me all about it one night in our cell. (Imagine going to sleep locked in a room with that guy. Of course, I stabbed a guy two dozen times, so I guess I would have made some people nervous, too.)

Another inmate later told me of his repeated rape of a girl he took on a date and decided that instead of dropping her off, he would drive to a secluded spot and rape her a few times. He was very smug and unapologetic about it. (These are the types of people I refer to when I speak of the haunting regret of not being able to hurt certain people that you come into contact with.) Another told the story of how a drug-addicted prostitute who was to testify against him was found in a field with a chunk of asphalt smashed into what used to be her head and how her killer was "never found." I looked into these men's eyes. I saw what they are capable of.

Of course, it began way before prison for me. I grew up around and was raised by very dangerous people. Even instances where violence *almost* happens can have a deep effect on your orientation, your understanding of how real violence is. I remember one time, particularly when I was maybe 16 or so. My uncle, Nowhere (as he was known), called me up and said he needed me to drive him to pick up his Harley. He was hit by a truck about two years prior, and while he was going through multiple surgeries and healing, he had been having his bike redone and hot-rodded. It was a badass shovelhead that was now punched out and double plugged, and the gold paint with the red SS lightning bolts on the tanks was all freshened up. It had been a while since he was ready to ride, but the bike shop was not getting the bike done, and he was pissed.

I showed up at his house and walked in to find him at the table, loading his 9mm. I said, *"Whoa, what the fuck are we doing?"*

I'm going to get my motherfucking scooter," he replied. Things hadn't been going well between him and the shop. He finished loading his pistol and grabbed a spare mag, and we climbed into his pristine 1977 Chrysler New Yorker Brougham 4-door (a gangster ass car I would still love to have to this day).

Nowhere had been a patched club member for many years, and he was an *old school* outlaw biker through and through. I trusted his lead and did what he told me to. When we arrived at the bike shop--a hardcore shop at a biker's house on the edge of the city that did a lot of work for the clubs in the area--my uncle's beautiful shovel was sitting in the drive, ready to go. It was uneventful and quick, and I climbed behind the wheel of that gigantic boat of a car and followed Nowhere back home.

I have no doubts that he would have pulled his pistol if it hadn't gone well. Of course, being family and having grown up in *the life*, I accepted those possibilities and agreed to back him up. It was just the way we did things. Nothing happened that time, but the potential was there, and it was a potential that my uncle and I were certain about. I am not sure if the bike shop owner really knew how close he was or what he himself had planned. But you didn't worry about that. You went prepared to do your work and planned to outwork the other guy. It was that simple.

But throughout my childhood, adolescence and young adulthood, there were plenty of times that the violence *did* occur. Sometimes I was present for the preparation and knew it was coming, and sometimes it was a surprise. Sometimes I was involved, and other times I was just a bystander. But the times where it almost happened make you wonder the most. How often have we been close to experiencing extreme violence, and we never even knew it?

Because of these experiences, I have no doubt whatsoever that dangerous people are literally all around my family and me all the time. It's a heavy burden to realize this in such a very personal way. If you don't have children or a family of your own, it may be easy because you don't really have anyone in your life that you truly fear losing, or you don't believe it will happen to you or them. But the moment you get a real glimpse of who's out there with us, it all changes. The fear sweeps in because not only do you know there are monsters that would hurt them, but you have seen and known these types of monsters personally. They are very real to me, much more so than some series you watched on Netflix or some news reports you saw on CNN. I lived with them for years. And as much as you may fail to understand it, I even became friends with some of them. I even loved some of them in my own family.

What's important to remember here is that the violent person you may have to deal with someday will likely have this type of personal understanding and close relationship with violence. You have to acknowledge that, and then you have to deal with it in multiple ways.

Realizing this, you will then need to re-balance yourself. You have to learn to compartmentalize fear and knowledge and work hard to find beauty in life as well. Romanticize the small things, and it helps to balance that threat. But most people will never reach that point because they can't deal with acknowledging the expansiveness of the threat itself. It's like when they walk on something really high and just close their eyes, *"just tell me when we're on the other side,"* they'll say. That is how they operate mentally going through life. *"Just don't look at it; it will go away; it won't happen to me."*

In my training classes, I often give the example of an active shooter shooting your baby, child, or wife first. Can you continue?

Imagine this deeply. You are with the ones you love the most, out in public, and shots ring out. A hand slips away from your grasp as your loved one--your child/wife/husband--falls lifeless to the floor with blood pooling around them. *What will you do?* Because you know you can not save them while you are being ripped apart by bullets, and you can not save your remaining loved ones if you are attending to the first one while the killer is still sending bullets into all of you.

You have to do one job and then the other. This is not an easy thing to be able to do. Many people who carry a gun, civilian, law enforcement and military alike, think they are prepared but would fall apart in such a scenario. You have to be able to look at the information coming in, analyze it, synthesize it, and move forward. In this instance, it would be nearly impossible to operate rapidly enough without an implicit guidance in place. A simple implicit guidance response would be, "I am being shot at; I have to stop the shooter." Your brain then employs your training to stop the shooter. Once that is done and the scene is safe from further apparent attack, you move to render aid.

This is a similar problem that can be faced by a member of a high-risk entry team, such as a violent fugitive task force in law enforcement or a special operations military unit operating in hostile environments overseas. Imagine making entry on a building that you believe houses mass murderers or violent militants. As you move through the blasted door frame and into the first room, the team member in front of you gets hit in the head and goes down at your feet. You personally saw the splatter from the hit as gravity dropped him suddenly to the floor, and you know immediately those are all definite signs of instant death.

You also know who he is. He is your friend. Your brother. You know his family. You celebrated birthdays with him and shared in his happiness when his new baby was born just earlier this year. You know his wife and how much she loves him.

At that split-second window of time, you have a choice. Do you push through, do your job, take over his job, and continue fighting forward to take down whatever attacker just killed him and is still trying to kill you and your teammates? Or do you fall apart, miss your steps, and become the second teammate out of the game, which exposes the remaining teammates to an even higher risk of death and failure?

Much of how these types of situations play out has to do with the stories we are telling ourselves about who we are and how we fit into the world around us. But it doesn't stop there. Stories and symbolism can only take you so far. It also has to do with our real capabilities and the confidence we have in those capabilities. Without personal experience or death-defying initiation, you are at a deficit here. Your performance is affected by your ability to have clarity concerning the incoming information and to not allow your biases and incestuous amplification to corrupt that information. I would argue that it all begins with acknowledging the reality that we do face the possibility of extreme violence and that violent people are present in every town and every city.

2:12. Issuing Force

It's been discussed at length in popular texts that humans are somehow averse to killing one another. When I first read this notion, I was long past my personal era of violence. Nonetheless, I was bewildered that such a notion could be held, let alone be held in such high regard. Had these experts never encountered killers in their "studies"? How could this be when I have personally known so many?

To be honest, I am fairly certain that I do know the answer to why highly-regarded or at least popular "experts" would have the view that humans would nearly always tend to posture rather than issue deadly force. I believe it has to do with the sample demographic used in such "studies" and interviews. I have seen evidence of this after entering into the professional training world and dealing with average civilians, law enforcement officers and military personnel.

The first time I encountered someone openly unwilling to use deadly force against another human being was in a class of civilians fulfilling requirements to get their concealed weapons permits. There, I encountered people who were scared for their safety but were also very non-violent in their nature and past experiences. It was actually a common enough dilemma that I had developed several techniques for dealing with it.

I remember one charming elderly lady who had attended the class with her husband. The pair were in their 80's and living in a neighborhood that had fallen victim to poverty like so many, probably a great place when they moved there 40 years ago but not a safe place today. You could tell they were deeply in love and probably had been married for 60 years or so. Her husband was a small, quiet guy, and she did most of the talking.

When the discussion of killing came up, she was forthright about her unwillingness to ever do it. I questioned her about it as a class discussion, even putting the criteria on her that the person would be trying to kill her. She didn't care; she still did not think she could use deadly force on someone, even if they were using deadly force on her.

Seeing how deeply in love they were, I asked her if she could do it in defense of her husband. I said, *"What if a bad guy was standing over him with a knife about to stab him, and you had your revolver a few feet away? Could you save him?"*

"Absolutely! I would shoot them to save him." Ok, this is progress. *"But you still wouldn't stop someone from hurting you if it meant you might kill them?"* She responded, *"No, I just couldn't do it."*

I then told her, *"You clearly love your husband, right? Now, think about this, imagine if something happened to you and you suddenly were not around anymore? Do you think that would hurt your husband?"*

"Yes, of course, it would," she responded.

I then told her, *"Imagine how incredibly sad he would be, missing you every day. And who would take care of him and make sure he is eating well and getting along OK? So, you see, you would be willing to save him directly from an attacker, but you wouldn't be willing to save him from the pain and loneliness of losing you and having to survive on his own for the rest of his lonely days?"*

It was at that moment that you could see the paradigm shift in her eyes. She got it. She understood, finally, that her life was more valuable than some criminal's life because people depended on her to be there. She ended up stating very convincingly that she would never let someone take her away from her husband. She went on to perform well enough in the course to be competent in at least defending herself and him in their home.

This was actually a commonly manifested psychological hurdle I would encounter with civilians. The majority of people who come to classes to either get weapon permits or to learn how to fight more effectively with weapons are largely peaceful people concerned with their family's safety from violent crime. It's a requirement of weapon permits issued by states that the individual be law-abiding, not be a prohibited felon, and not have domestic violence convictions. So, it stands to reason that you are not going to be filling classes with street-hardened killers. These are a demographic of people who mostly have lived outside of criminal violence (aside from a few violence survivor outliers).

Most of these people will not have anything resembling an orientation developed for violence, issuing force, or performing under force pressure. Their propensity to kill is typically going to be very low, if not nonexistent altogether. Their tendency to posture against a violent threat (e.g., brandish a gun or fire a warning shot) will be high. All of this, of course, is not suitable for defense against a deadly force attack.

Another story comes to mind, which was told to me by an officer I personally know. He had a suspect swinging a gun towards him, and even though he had the suspect's head in front of his muzzle at a near-point blank distance, he did not pull the trigger.

As he tells it, he engaged with the suspect in a residence's front yard. This was one of those old, two-story Midwest homes with the big, raised front porch. They ended up against the front porch with him on top of the suspect, who was crouched in front of him and facing away. The officer, a younger guy who regularly trains at a high level, drew his weapon as he sees the suspect reaching underneath him, and he won't comply with the *"Show me your hands!"* command.

Right then, the suspect begins to swing around and up towards the officer, and he clearly has a handgun in his hand. The officer had already completed his draw and pointed his weapon at the suspect's head. He did not fire.

The suspect's weapon luckily hit the bottom of the porch on the way up, which disrupted the swing towards the officer, who then pounced on the suspect and took control of his weapon hand. He was able to subdue the suspect with a muzzle shoved into the back of his head and lots of threats of blowing his head off.

The average citizen or juror may think that was a good arrest since no deadly force was used. But those of us who understand fighting, that officer included, know that it was 100% luck that the suspect swung into that porch. If he had completed that turn towards the officer, that officer would not have had the time to make the decision to defend himself by neutralizing the suspect. It would have been too late. That officer is haunted by his hesitancy to pull the trigger that day. While he is glad he didn't have to, he knows that it was pure luck that he was not shot because of his inability to act against a suspect actively swinging a handgun towards him to attack. He confesses that he does not know why he didn't do it. He hopes that he never makes that mistake when it will cost him his life.

If you were to interview the survivors of violent attacks and those survivors happened to be concealed weapon permit holders, you would be pooling data from this demographic. Since the police and military also have requirements for their entrants to be law-abiding and not have felonies or violent records, you can see how they would come from a similar non-violent background to a large extent (though not totally, there are no absolutes in this context).

Perhaps this is where the misconceptions about the human nature of killing came from? I can only speculate. Or, maybe it stems from the work of S.L.A. Marshall, who influenced Army manuals and popular books with his (now known to be) fabricated statistics and "facts." He made claims that only *15% of returning combat vets in WWII reported firing their weapons during combat.* Somehow eventually, it was concluded that this meant that 85% had acted upon their *aversion* to firing on another human being despite being in a firefight. And while Marshall made many other claims that have been disputed or proven outright false, I just want to focus on the firing rate of soldiers because it alone has influenced popular texts on the subject, and it just is not accurate.

98

These "ratios" were not gathered from empirical data. Marshall did not conduct any empirical research. There is no such defined research or resultant data attributed to Marshall in the possession of the Army *or anywhere else, for that matter.* He created the basis for others to come along and claim that humans must be conditioned thoroughly to fire upon another human with intentional lethal force. Again, this simply is not accurate *on its face.*

Now, speaking to the more modern interviews conducted with combat vets and law enforcement officers who have participated in combat or firefights, I refer to the examples I set forth above from my concealed weapons classes and the officer who didn't shoot when he had every reason to.

The premise seems to be that humans need specific conditioning and training to kill one another, and even with that, it does not always result in a willingness to kill. I disagree. We have been killing each other since the dawn of time. In fact, in some places of the world, it is still a part of the culture. The law-abiding, largely non-violent "good guy" population may require some conditioning to bring them to the point of the intentional application of lethal force. That, I agree with. But to attribute this to all humans, as in our human nature, is not to murder each other? As in, the bad guy isn't likely to be willing to kill you? Who comes up with this shit?

If it is intentional conditioning that is needed, then the "bad guys" don't need any because they already get their conditioning from their natural life circumstances. They do not require any special conditioning to create the orientation for lethal force. Under no circumstances would I believe that claims like "humans inherently don't want to hurt each other" would be anything close to accurate.

I know that, at least in the world that I spent my youth and young adulthood, humans not only do not have an aversion to killing one another, they sometimes will do so quite enthusiastically. No, it is not a characteristic always caused by some mental illness. You just have to interview the right demographic.

Speaking from experience, I can assure you that as an 18-year-old, kid I *did not* have an aversion to killing someone. Do you think that when I plunged my knife blade into another man's body a total of two dozen times that I was at all posturing? Or would you assume that I had malice in my heart, even if I was acting in self-defense? My beliefs about the event, coupled with my beliefs about who he was and about who I was, all drove that intent from deep within.

He *"deserved it,"* he initiated the conflict and went out of his way to pursue and assault me. I was *"good,"* he was *"bad,"* which made him the villain, the bad guy, the *terrorist.* Right or wrong, that story was in play. My value was raised, his was grossly depreciated, and I operated out of *righteousness.* He was quite simply the bad guy, and I didn't care one bit for his well-being in the process of me stopping him from hurting me.

The stories we tell ourselves and that help shape our orientation are what can tip humans over the edge from posturing to the intent to kill with malice, completely devoid of aversion. In my case, I *knew* I was a *victim,* I had tried many times to avoid the confrontation, and I knew he deliberately and repeatedly sought the confrontation out. This, in my mind, *absolved me of guilt* and freed me to act with malice in the vicious defense of my life. It is what drove my actions. I had belief, I had justification, and I had the means. It was *simply a choice*, not a moral dilemma.

From another angle, when my father would become enraged and strangle me as a young teen, I could see in his fiery eyes that he, without any doubt, had what it took to kill me. And many a time, I thought he was doing just that, especially in his drunken rage. While that may be considered a crime of passion, and he may only have had the propensity to kill me during a session of rage, what resulted in me was, alternatively, a willingness to kill him that was present in my calmest state. I would often think of murdering him in his sleep, and sometimes today marvel at how intently I did think about that as a young teenage boy. That type of conditioning is present in the lives of many of the youth in our nation today.

There is no doubt that events like these shaped my willingness to use deadly force on another human whom I had deemed deserving of it, cultivating it by a very early age. It is events like that shaping the narrative of the development of violent orientations in the criminal population. There's no rhyme or reason to how some people turn out to be violent from such exposures, while another kid can grow up in the exact same home and turn out completely passive. Nor can we explain the kids who come from balanced, loving homes yet go on to become vicious murderers. That's beyond my capabilities to explain, and I would argue beyond the capabilities of science in its current form to be able to explain.

What we can explain is that in individuals who have not manifested obvious mental illnesses but have grown to be ultra-violent and efficient at violent or predatory behaviors, we can often see where the components of their orientation have been shaped by their experiences, their culture, and the stories they have created about who they are and how they fit into the world around them. This is information we can use.

This is why I have emphasized the importance of our personal mythos and the dangers of incestuous amplification and justification by righteousness throughout this book. These are the deep-seated information sets that will influence our decision-making and mean the difference between winning and losing and the difference between going home and going to prison or worse.

2:13. Facing the Aftermath

Almost anyone can be trained to perform specific skills and procedures in defense against violence. They can even be trained to a nearly automatic level of skill performance, working off cues to deliver deadly violence in the face of an attack. What is not easy to train is the psychological structure and integrity to deal with a life-altering violent event after it has happened.

The consequences of such an event can be devastating. This is easily exhibited in the vast examples of PTSD in soldiers returning from combat and attempting to reorient back into this world. In this world, killing and artillery are not everyday occurrences. I have pretty strong beliefs that it is between the orientation going in and the attempt to return to that orientation afterward that may be responsible for so much psychological trauma. The trauma is primarily in the form of moral injury.

Again, I am no expert, and I sure as hell am not a psychologist. (I also don't have much trust that some non-violent academic will understand those of us who come from a violent world with violent paradigm shifts, either.) What I *can* speak about is my own experiences and the experiences that a few close people in my life have shared with me about this phenomenon.

Like those soldiers, I also was very young when I was sent into the cruel world of the U.S. prison system. Having just turned 19, my young mind was bombarded with the brutality and predatory ways that would literally be the rules of my life for five whole years. I had to learn a whole new way of thinking, of seeing, of acting. I had to adjust my entire awareness level to what would have seemed superhuman before prison. You literally become so good at reading individuals and groups' behavior and the feel of the environment that you can predict events before they become evident.

And the violence. The violence changes you; it changes your brain. Seeing human beings beaten to death, stabbed to death, or locked in cages covered in their own piss and feces, screaming mad. Watching young men being sexually abused or forced into human trafficking within the prison. That changes how you see the world, how you see other human beings.

Soldiers have informed me of very similar experiences when they encounter how people live in some of these third-world countries they go into, such as seeing children starved to death or sold into slavery. One soldier told me of witnessing the sexual abuse of a young male child by a group of locals who deemed it admissible behavior in their culture. The federal government bound him not to engage or entangle into the locals' culture they were infiltrating, so he was forced to turn the other way. Just like in prison, you have reasons that you can not and will not intervene. It's how life is there, and people who haven't been there can't understand that or the potential moral injury that comes with it.

Circling back to the immediate topic at hand, facing the aftermath of an initiation event, it's important to keep in mind that the "good guy" I have spoken of here--the one who didn't grow up in an environment that acclimated his orientation to violence and a casual or *utilitarian* devaluation of human life over many years and from a young age-- typically experiences the initiation quite rapidly. This is where the largest difference occurs between how the two opposing sides develop their orientation. That rapid transition of culture shock and reorientation into a new and brutal world with deadly consequences can be debilitating for a person of good moral character and values to withstand.

It's the exact same thing I witness happen with the unlucky people who are not really criminals and not violent but happened to get sentenced to prison. They are mentally not prepared to shift their values that drastically and that rapidly. When it happens, it is quite a violent psychological event that can cause a lot of trauma. Suppose you have general compassion for people and maybe even a desire to help others,

104

when you are forced to watch terrible things happen to innocent or defenseless people, you can be seriously, morally injured. In that case, you are damaged at a moral level.

When you are forced to participate in those events, like a soldier forced to fire on a child carrying a weapon or IED, you are morally injured in often irreversible ways. The change is too drastic and too abrupt. You were not adequately prepared at a cultural level. Your values were not adjusted before the event, and you will very often suffer through that instant change.

On the other side of the tracks, the violent criminal or the enemy combatant has developed differently. They've grown up in a war zone or in a criminal environment marked by poverty, death and personal loss. They've grown up watching children suffer abuse, starvation and slavery. They've had years of losing their friends and relatives to violence, be it criminal murder or warfare, and they have acclimated to the adjusted values of human life. Many of them have accepted their fate (again, recalling Tupac's lyrics here) and are prepared to die young

"Or you can send me to hell cuz I ain't begging for my life. Ain't nothing worse than this cursed ass hopeless life. I'm troublesome." (Tupac, *Troublesome '96*)

As we can see in the street soldier culture, death is not only unavoidable; it is glorified. Memento Mori isn't something they have on a challenge coin, it's a mindset they may not even know they have, but they do. When soldiers face enemy combatants in foreign lands, those combatants often have cultural belief systems in place for this very mechanism as well. The infamous "72 virgins" is an often-cited example of this.

Whatever it is, the culture, value system, and experiences all accumulate into a powerful orientation towards violence and the devaluation of human life. It happens over many years and often begins at a very early age. It sets in over time and becomes hardened, reinforced.

Facing the aftermath of a traumatic event can be costly and difficult, even if you are thoroughly prepared and acquainted with that type of trauma. It can cause problems even if you feel one hundred percent OK with it in your waking life. I can offer my own example of how I suffered for the first several years after my release from prison.

Now, I can say that prison wasn't a terrible experience for me. I wasn't maimed, killed, raped, or abused in any significant way (outside of how the system is designed to abuse you, of course). I fared way better than many kids my age. I was better prepared than they were, both in culture and experience.

But that did not save me from PTSD and severe after-effects. For many years I would have terrible nightmares where I was being attacked or murdered. Because I had been present and even participated in these types of events in real life, the nightmares were incredibly vivid. These were *active* nightmares, meaning I would come out of bed swinging and kicking and fighting for my fucking life, right out of a dead sleep.

The worst time I remember happened within the first year of being out. I woke up tangled up in my bedsheet on my kitchen floor. The table and chairs were knocked over and broken. A pot of grease was slung from the stovetop all over the ceiling, cupboards and floor. If you read Violence of Mind, you read about one incident where a kid snapped and tried to kill me in my sleep, so this problem was due to real shit happening and from seeing it happen to other people firsthand.

The interesting thing is, I didn't live with *fear*. I wasn't consciously walking around during the day in fear of being attacked in my sleep. Nor was I suffering any noticeable traumatic responses during my waking life. But the trauma found a backdoor to my mind through sleep and attacked me there. Very often, the trauma and its effects are inescapable. And I was someone who was fairly well acclimated to extreme violence and oriented to it quite well.

The delicate balance is finding the safe line between preparing yourself to deal with such trauma while retaining your ability to be a good human and still have compassion for others. This is why I push the idea of professionalism when it comes to violence. This involves the compartmentalization of our attachments and values so that we can focus on the task at hand. It also involves the thorough evaluation and adjustment of those values before that time comes. It's the preparation for reorientation back into your normal world, but with your new paradigm. This new knowledge and set of capabilities you now live with is the real challenge.

The point here is the after-effects are not corrected fully when it happens. That is too late. The aftermath is prepared for systematically, at a cultural level, before it happens. Then, you will experience the consequences for well after it happened (maybe, or in some way). If you come from a "good" life, one void of the terror of the worst humankind has to offer, and you venture into a job that brings you into contact with that terrible world, your initiation *will* come.

You may also experience it as just an average person who finds yourself under attack someday by random selection. Whether it makes you or breaks you is largely determined by your preparation. Still, in totality, it is determined by your culture, values, attachments, parameters (internal/external), experience, confidence, your ability to synthesize new Information and, lastly, your genetics. Don't just prepare for the event. Prepare to re-enter life after the event. That is the true completion of an initiation process: the *coming back* .

Section III:

Operating Outward

3:1 Perception: The Other Piece of Orientation

You can not effectively accomplish anything outwardly if you are entirely focused inward. You can not protect yourself from a violent attack by focusing inwardly on the fear of dying, or your will to live, or the fear of missing your family. You must focus outwardly to be able to do the work to change the circumstances that are threatening those attachments. This is the whole premise of O.O.D.A., of Sun Tzu's Art of War, and of Musashi's martial strategies (and the works of countless other conflict strategists), to force the opponent to turn his focus inward towards his fears and attachments, to doubt his plans and abilities and to accumulate negative mental imagery while our focus is on him. Let us take a deeper look.

Robert Coram, in his book *Boyd: The Fighter Pilot who changed the Art of War*, precisely stated, *"Sun Tzu, a Chinese military theoretician, was thought to have written The Art of War about 400 B.C. Sun Tzu's ideas about conflict include such themes as deception, speed, fluidity of action, surprise, and shaping the adversary's perception of the world."* That last part is of monumental importance to us here. To quote Miyamoto Musashi, directly from *The Book of Five Rings* (Wilson, 2002), *"Observation and perception are two separate things; the observing eye is stronger, the perceiving eye is weaker."*

What happens between observation and perception? A series of factors come into play where a person tries to interpret and understand what they see through the analysis and synthesis of information as it feeds into their orientation. This is where mistakes are made, and our perceptions are colored by our fears, attachments, experience or lack thereof, and our cultural inputs and values. This is where incestuous amplification takes place. This is equally true for both you and your enemy. Men of violence deeply understood this 2400 years ago, as evidenced by Musashi's writings and the works of other ancient martial strategists.

Perception can be manipulated and even fully created, using concealment, false cues, probing, deception and misdirection. It happens in interpersonal relationships, and it happens in major social events like elections. A great example of this is seen in the movie *Our Brand is Crisis* (the 2005 documentary about the Bolivian election, not the Hollywood movie of the same name that came later). The documentary shows in detail the process of campaign marketing by famous political strategists that market politicians like they are products being "sold" to a population. That's a scary concept if you think about it. Nonetheless, it is absolutely true and is what happens at election time.

From criminals to conmen, magicians to circus sideshow operators, and from corporate marketing professionals to political marketing strategists, the management of perceptions has been an art and fieldcraft for hundreds of years, if not thousands.

In the previous section, we covered the inward operations of managing our own perceptions of ourselves, others and the world around us. Now we'll look at the many ways that one would manage the perception of others around them.

3:2 Predatory Skill: Fooling Perception, Intuition and Instinct

The highest level of fieldcraft for any predator is to be able to fool the perception and instincts of an aware prey. You can see this in action everywhere, from the animals of the jungles and forests to the human predators and their prey in prisons and on the streets of our cities. Anyone can sneak up on a deeply sleeping prey, but not every predator can get close to the prey that is aware, listening and expecting the predator to show up. Yet, it still happens every single day.

Science can not accurately define "instinct" or identify its origins in an organism. We can be sure of this: human behaviors all range from being modifiable to very rigid. This can be seen on a species level, and it can be seen on an individual level. Rather than trying to pretend we are super smart by using a bunch of big science words, let's talk about this in terms we can both understand and observe. For our purposes here, we will say that instincts are innate and hardwired into us. Whether they come from 50,000 years ago or the last five generations plus our inherited environment...we'll let the academics argue about that.

We all have *prey* instincts embedded deeply within us. We are inherently this way because for the first ten to fifteen years of our lives; we are literally incapable of being self-sufficient, fully dependent upon someone else for our sustenance and safety. As infants and toddlers, we are purely prey, completely incapable of our own protection and in most cases not able to detect threats at all. Someone has to protect us, and that means they have to recognize, at least on a subconscious level, that we are merely potential prey. Man has been prey for many thousands of years. Every human spends at least a part of their life as defenseless prey, and many spend their whole life in that condition.

I find it very interesting that some humans develop very recognizable predator instincts. They can sense when someone is vulnerable. Some may argue that this is more a function of intuition and is a purely learned behavior, but I am not so sure of that after having known and observed so many predators in very close, personal ways. Some people will prey on others' weaknesses and seemingly not even know they are doing it. For them, it is as naturally triggered as the "chase instinct" in a dog or wolf. The prey runs, the animal gives chase, and it is not totally a conscious decision; it's simply hardwired into them.

Most of us can relate to the idea of getting a "gut feeling" about a certain place or person when something inexplicably gives us a sense of impending danger if we proceed or stay in the company that we are in. The brain has matched up some predetermined amount of red flags and has sent the body an alarm. I always suggest listening to those "gut feelings" because they are usually right in some way. Gavin De Becker, in his book *The Gift of Fear*, outlines this pretty well, *"intuition is always right in at least two important ways; It is always in response to something, it always has your best interest at heart."*

Intuition is defined as the ability to understand, know or consider a thing likely without exclusively using conscious reasoning. Intuition is not a "sixth sense" or some type of spirit magic. Unlike instinct, it is not rigid and can be modified by learning and experience. Intuition is simply the brain's ability to recognize and respond to information and patterns without having to involve your conscious thoughts too much, if at all. Think of it like an antivirus program running on your computer; just because you can't see it working does not mean it isn't there. It's running and scanning in the background, sometimes dormant, sometimes sending alerts.

There are several ways to defeat the instincts and intuition of prey. You should know these, both as potential prey and as potential defenders looking to defeat an attacking opponent (in which case, I would argue that you must act as a predator yourself.

3:3 Concealment

Concealment is arguably the most powerful tool in the fieldcraft of perception management. Throughout this book, we have already talked about it in many different ways, and I covered it heavily in *Violence of Mind*. Concealment is instrumental in the manipulation of O.O.D.A. and in disrupting the opponent's plans. It is used in the creation of personal mythos and self-imaging. The predator employs it in concert with impression management to fool victims into a disadvantaged position. They conceal who they really are while managing the impression they want you to have, as we will discuss later in this book. Most basically, it is used to hide weapons and tools.

For the defender or the hunter, it is ultimately what can be used to turn the situation around when you have been ambushed or caught off guard and desperately need any advantages you can get.

A person cannot prepare for, nor react to, a threat that they do not yet know exists. When you are the one who must react--as in you are not initiating the attack but are being or about to be attacked--your goal is to present a counter threat that they cannot fully detect and not anticipate. It can not be a purely predictable reaction because you want them to be overwhelmed when they realize it is happening. When the prey is themselves a predator as well or inherently has the same capabilities as the attacking predator like we humans do, the stakes are much higher for the attacker, so concealment and timing become the *high arts* of the experienced.

Concealment fieldcraft is the concealing of tools, intentions and capabilities. It is as much concealing your personality, what you are thinking, what you are planning and what you are capable of as it is hiding a gun or knife under your shirt. It is a full fieldcraft within itself, and the experienced criminal is extremely good at it on all levels. None of the other tools used in fooling the instincts or intuition of prey will work without the mastering of concealment *first*.

Concealment is also the first component of perception management. First, the actor conceals what they really are or what is really happening in the environment; then, the actor projects cues conclusive to what they want others to think they are. This is why it is important to understand it, both from the giving and receiving ends.

In nature, concealment is witnessed in both physical features and behaviors: The mountain lion blends into the weeds and sits motionless because she knows that the slightest movement will alert any prey of her presence. The rattlesnake that sits just under a hollowed log on the edge of a path, out of sight but able to see his strike path to grab unsuspecting prey. These are obvious behaviors and tools used universally among animals and humans alike.

Among humans, that concealment can be visual and behavioral as well. A developed predator knows that certain clothing will cue off prey. He knows better than to approach with his dirty hoodie pulled up around his face and his hands in his pockets if his goal is to get close to you with your guard down. He is not dumb. He is highly evolved. He knows that his language and demeanor will indicate where he may be from and what he is capable of. A thug talking in foul street language can be a menacing threat, while being soft-spoken, articulate, and even having witty humor can be totally disarming. Both are choices; they are not involuntary behaviors. Any person can choose to be nice or choose to be scary. The scary person can choose to be friendly, and that is what is important here.

You will often hear someone say, *"He's so charming!"* as if it is a character trait. But is he? Or is he *choosing* to be charming? And if he is choosing to be charming, the question is, why is he choosing to do so at this moment? Sure, it could very well be because he chooses to live his life as a nice, helpful guy. But it could also be a chosen behavior that is designed to manipulate your perception of him to get closer to you so he can access a resource from you. People do exactly this in romantic or intimate relationships all the time, and many still fall for it.

I remember when I fell for it not too long ago when I joined a local gym. The sales guy was quite a talker, and he really inflated my ego when he commented on how intense I was and how my experience was impressive. He asked many questions about me, who I am, where I come from, what I do for work. He listened and then praised and made a big deal out of the info he gathered. He even grabbed one of his female co-workers as she walked by and said, *"Hey! This guy right here is the real deal! He does some badass stuff!"*

He made me feel respected, even revered a little. He put me on a pedestal. I bought the membership, of course. Sure, I predetermined that I wanted it before I went in that day, but he certainly had me sold that my experience there would be great based on how I was treated going into the door. He made me feel special and definitely someone he would never forget. I paid the money and signed the contract; I was in.

About a week later, I get a call from this same sales guy. Did he want to ask how my membership was going? Did he want to tell me how much he remembered about me? Nope. He was TRYING TO SELL ME A MEMBERSHIP!! This son-of-a-bitch was straight up asking me if I was ready to consider coming back in to sign up for that membership I had inquired about. I even tried to jog his memory and asked him, *"You don't remember me, do you? The coach just looking for a spot to work out locally?"* I said.

"Sure, I remember you! That's why I wanted to know if you were ready to get signed up and get started!" he responded.

"Dude, you already signed me up a week ago. You already got a commission off of me, and you made me think you were like my biggest fan. I signed up the day I came in, and YOU are the one who sold me the membership. But you are obviously a poor salesman because your actions only go as deep as getting the next sale, then the customer gets

pushed on down the line, and you immediately forget about them. You are full of shit, and no one should believe a word that comes out of your mouth, you cheeseball."

That's pretty much what I told him. He concealed the fact that his words and flattery were purely motivated by a quick sale and were not remotely true. (He got me, but in the end, he got himself because anyone who operates that way is found out in short order.) He acutely picked up on the story I was telling myself, that I was somewhat of a humble badass, and he fucking played it to the max.

I was miffed that I fell for it, but then again, I knew the stakes were a membership to a gym I wanted into anyway, so perhaps my radar didn't need to be on high. Would I be so relaxed with a guy flattering me in a dark alley? Most definitely not. It's quite fatiguing to walk around on high alert all day, every day, and in every interaction you have with people. Knowing the difference between when to turn it on and when to relax is part of the learning process. Just know, in little ways, you're going to get "got" here and there.

But here is an interesting part of this story. I profiled this guy as well, in retrospect. During our sales meeting, he also shared his own story. He was a former drug addict and convicted felon who turned his life around and found God. He now devoted his life to ministry and helping others. He even showed me an article in a local magazine about him and his *life-changing story*. He had a disfigured leg from a K-9 unit getting a hold of him during an arrest and tearing the shit out of his lower leg.

Looking back, after he had revealed the shallow nature of his personality and motives, I was able to retrospectively decipher this guy's story that he is struggling to tell himself. I say struggling because he reeked of desperation, a particular brand of desperation that I had seen before in "jailhouse religion." He was a guy who obviously had serious issues, had been a terrible drug addict and probably had burnt most people in his life. He was fighting a battle to prove to the world and,

120

most of all, to himself that he was changed, that he was worth something as a man and a human. The poor guy was doing his best with what he had to work with. It still didn't change the fact that he's a cheeseball salesman that has as much bullshit in his pitch now as I'm sure he did when he was a low-level drug addict running game on his family and friends. I picked up on a lot of this during our initial meeting but chose to let my ego get stroked by my desire to be accepted into this new gym in a new town. We all have a story to tell...

While salesmen and predatory dates are a nuisance, violent criminals and combatants are dangerous, and they employ these tools and strategies perhaps better than most. The major difference with them is that you don't simply get your heart broken or your wallet lightened. With them, you can get seriously hurt and even raped or murdered.

The information provided by appearance, demeanor, dress, and so on can be used to mislead and even to incite false cues in someone. A less capable predator may appear tougher and more menacing than they really are to incite fear and compliance in their victim. Conversely, they could be a serial killer that appears completely harmless, as many of them do.

But we must know that it is entirely possible to fool the powerful warning systems of intuition and instinct. We should know that some people have perfected the art of doing so. And we should know that it is a skill set we need to at least partially develop in ourselves if we want to counter such predatory behavior someday.

A great example of this is the girl who became the rape victim of the inmate I spoke of in the *Facing the reality of violence* part of a previous chapter. The guy drove her to a remote location instead of driving her home as she intended. Let's think about this for a moment. During that drive, at some point, she had to get at least the feeling that something was off. Perhaps she didn't want to panic or seem irrational by reacting poorly (often an issue with females and their inability to enforce boundaries).

But if she did realize she may be in danger, she would have had a few choices. The primary choice is when to act on the danger. In other words, when should she take an action that will give away the fact that she knows she is in danger, which will then alert the predator that the prey knows and is looking for an escape? If she alerts him at the wrong time, like after they arrive at the remote location, he will be able to contain her easily and not let her get away. If she alerts him too early, he may escalate and drive faster, making escape impossible while he grows more desperate and, consequently, more dangerous.

However, if she employed concealment and deception and managed the perception of her attacker by remaining calm or even somewhat compliant, like "Sure, let's take a ride, it's ok," she would disarm his senses and not give him a reason to accelerate the timeline of the attack, nor would he be urged to grow more desperate or aggressive. This would allow her to choose when to act, making it a complete surprise to the predator.

A good strategy would have been to remain calm and compliant nonchalantly and then bailing out of the car explosively at the next stop sign, traffic signal, or even slow down point. She would be choosing the location of her separation rather than him choosing the location of their destination. He would be fooled into thinking he had her tricked until she was out of the car and running away from danger, perhaps even screaming and causing a scene.

But this requires thought, experience and maybe even some training on how to **listen to your own instincts and intuition and then to conceal those instinctual and intuitive responses from those who seek to harm or manipulate you.** Either way, if you want to go against the predator successfully, you need to have access to the same tools and skills that will be used against you. You are both human and both susceptible to the same methods and tricks.

3:4 Cueing off of Others

Another skill in detecting or fooling instinct and intuition is the ability to cue off others' responses to the environment. As De Becker points out, *"When free of judgment, we inherently respect the intuition of others. Sensing that someone else is in that special state of assessing hazard, we are alerted, just as when we see the cat or dog awaken suddenly from a nap and stare intently into a dark hallway."*

This is an interesting one in the context of prison since the cues others give off can be either natural or by design to solicit a specific reaction. Often, telling the difference is very difficult. As an inmate, you become very attuned to how others treat you, look at you, and act around you. You are constantly scanning for threats, especially in the beginning, so you are learning the behaviors, body language and inflections of the people around you in a way most people never do.

An example would be: You wake up on a given Saturday in the prison. Nothing is happening in your environment that would change the inmates' attitudes or behaviors. It's a normal, leisurely weekend day. But you notice something different. Someone looks at you a little differently, just for a split second. Do they know something? Hmm. Then it happens again, with a different person. The next thing you notice is some people seem to be avoiding you. Not being outright mean but diplomatically too *busy* to talk to you.

Nothing is overtly out of place, but these tiny changes in behaviors tell you something is going on, but you can't place anything specific. You venture out to breakfast and then to the yard for some sunshine and exercise.

Once on the yard, you notice the others are not as social as they would normally be and are staying tighter in their respective groups. There's a weird tension in the air, and you can *feel* it. What's going on?

It's not long before you get your answer. A commotion erupts about 30 yards to your right, and you look to find two groups engaged in a fierce battle. Several men have one unfortunate guy pinned to the ground, and he is being stabbed by multiple guys. They stab him between 50 and 100 times, and he dies in absolute terror on the ground of a prison yard alone.

What is learned from this? What cues from others did you pick up, and how accurate was it? Were the others simply picking up on cues from the would-be participants and then passing those cues on? Or were you seeing the actual participants acting differently?

If the observer is a predator, he will seek to understand what went wrong and why he was cued off so early. He makes mental notes, often unconsciously, about how to do it better when he needs to act someday. This will happen even if he was not involved in today's attack because he may have to use those same skills and tactics someday, and he will need to be successful; his life may depend on it. He will use that learned information to better fool or guide others with cues that he can employ himself or solicit in others.

If you are more of a prey or thinking in terms of being a potential target of such an attack someday, you will also take notes and adjust your intuition about others' cues. What can you do to pick up on such cues earlier? Is there any way to look back and think about whether you saw the victim in any interactions earlier that day? Were people treating him differently? How can you use others' behavioral changes to signal not only early general warnings but also to gather specific information?

To add perspective, the reason convicts acted differently that day stems from a few events. If there is to be a hit, there is actually a pretty decent amount of people who will know about it, at least generally. They may not know the specific target or time, but they will know a hit is going to happen. This causes a chain reaction since others will be highly tuned in to their environment for all of the reasons I explained earlier.

They will at least detect the tension among small groups, and that will, in turn, become tension that they emanate outward.

There's also that *gut feeling* thing that happens. As inexplicable as it is, there will be those who simply *pick up* on a tension in the environment without any consciously acknowledged cues. We've probably all experienced this without having a conscious reason for it. But there are reasons your brain did see or perceive things that alerted you to change your behavior. And then someone else picks up on that behavior change. It can be other innocent people, or it can be the predator that sees that change in you.

Just remember that the behavior of others can be involuntary or voluntary. It can be unconsciously driven by instinct or intuition. It can be designed by someone who understands how to fool instinct and intuition by mimicking it or causing others to experience it falsely.

3:5 Probing

A technique often used by predators, but one that can be useful to prey as well, is probing. Probing is taking any action to probe someone into giving out useful information. In this sense, that information will be specifically about vulnerabilities, theirs or yours.

Just about everyone has experienced the cigarette "opener" probe that some bums will use to ask for money. They'll approach and ask if you have a cigarette, but then if you answer or behave in a way that signals to them that you are open or approachable again, they will ask for money or something more specific. This is an elementary version of probing, but it's one that most people can recognize. In a low-level predatory sense, it's their way of avoiding an initial rejection of the thing they really want.

However, when dealing with truly dangerous predators, the stakes will be much higher, and the fieldcraft will be of a much higher level. The probing will be done with concealment, with the intention of not tripping off your instincts or intuition. They will also be tuned in enough to know that they can not behave in any way that will raise the tension in the environment, which will prevent you from passively picking up on cues from others, should you miss the danger yourself.

To draw another example from the predator's training grounds, prison, you will be probed as soon as you hit the door. Many predators with desires ranging from financial extortion to sexual exploitation will be searching for your weaknesses and vulnerabilities.

I'll remind you here that just because you don't intend on going to prison doesn't mean that this is not important to you. If you will someday have to deal with a developed ex-convict, you will need this information. These same individuals will someday be released into your cities and neighborhoods, and you may have to deal with them.

Sometimes probing is a long, drawn-out process. Probing can precede a "grooming" process in relationship abuse or human trafficking situations. Take the classic abusive relationship, for example. If the abuser gets away with it, they will keep doing it. It can be emotional or physical. But if the victim keeps letting them get away with it, the abuser continues to receive the signals that it is acceptable and permitted for them to do it. How they learn what is permissible or tolerated is by probing, trying a little at a time, learning the victim's vulnerabilities and weaknesses that they will use to hold them hostage.

The abuser will give them what they think they need, but in reality, they have probed the victim so well that they have learned a literal map of their weaknesses and how to navigate them. All of this information is gathered from probing and from studying the responses the victim has to actions taken against them (arguably a form of probing itself).

Probing is used to defeat instincts and intuition. Testing your boundaries, the predator will gently find a way in without triggering your alert system. Even if you are guarded, there will always be a magical set of words, behaviors and appearances that will disarm your guard. The developed predator is constantly polishing his or her ability to perfect those behaviors. In this way, probing becomes one of the predator's most important tools, and it is a subset of the fieldcraft of concealment.

As a defender or someone who hunts predators, you will find probing to be just as useful for all of the same reasons. I emphasize here that you have to remove the negative connotations from the concept and know that it is just a useful tool. Whether it is used for good or bad is non-consequential to its usefulness. When faced with a dangerous predator, it is within your ability--and your obligation--to be just as deceptive to them as they would be to you.

Of course, the danger of probing is alerting the target of the probe or otherwise disrupting their behavior, also known as the

Heisenberg effect. The Heisenberg effect refers to those research occasions in which the very act of measurement or observation directly alters the phenomenon under investigation. This means that in the process of probing, you cause the target to alter their behavior in some way, possibly changing their intentions in the moment completely, which would defeat the purpose of covert manipulation. The purpose of covert manipulation, such as probing for boundaries or information, is to gather intel from a target without disturbing the behavior or awareness of the target. The avoidance of such disruption allows the information gained to be used by the predator, positioning themselves in any of a number of available advantages with predictable outcomes.

Such skills are not just for "bad guys," you could easily replace "predator" with agent, officer or operator, and the skills still apply. As one masters these capabilities over others, one finds out what his or her moral makeup really is.

3:6 Deception and Misdirection

As alluded to up to this point, a predator will use concealment, cues, and probing to deceive and misdirect a targeted victim's decision-making process. This can become a finely polished skill set that can absolutely fool the most alert victim's instincts and intuition. This is who you must prepare for. But more importantly, these are capabilities you should understand and gain for yourself to use against such an enemy. Whether you are a civilian who carries a weapon to protect yourself and your family, an officer who has to operate in violent neighborhoods, or a soldier who must interact with the local population where combatants hide in plain sight, these skills will be necessary for your success.

I recall a time as a teenager when I was maybe 14 or so years old, where all of this was used against me to set me up for a pretty serious attack. I was at home when a girl knocked on the door and asked me to come hang out with her and her friends. The girl was a former girlfriend that grew up around the corner from me, so I had some trust for her. The two guys in the car were known troublemakers, but I hadn't had any direct contact with them before. She assured me that everyone was cool, and she really wanted me to come, drink some beers and hang out with her. It was one of the guys' car, not hers. Typical for young me, like a lamb to the slaughter, I followed the cute girl to the car, and we took off.

We ended up in a wooded area the next town over, in a very isolated spot away from any view of the road and beyond a distance where someone would hear a scream. I don't recall if this alerted me or not, but it should have. Of course, I had one thing on my mind, so my instincts were being overridden by other biological instincts, to put it plainly. We had a beer or two, and then things turned violent.

Now, these two assholes were fucking huge. I mean, together, they had to clock in somewhere between 500 to 600 pounds—two big, strong country boys from the outskirts of town. The biggest one grabbed me and started to beat the shit out of me. I had no weapons, so I used the one thing I had that they didn't: speed. I broke free and ran like a motherfucker into the woods. This led me into a marsh wetland that I had to trudge through for about half a mile or more, including crossing a major interstate in a very dangerous and illegal way. My objective was to hide and getaway.

I emerged from the woods back in my town, soaked and muddy, and had to walk the streets another few miles to get home. I kept my eyes open and was prepared for them to find me at any time when I would simply run again because I knew their fat, sloppy asses weren't going to catch me.

Was the girl in on it? Or did they use her as bait and deceive her into doing it? I will never know for sure, but I was always inclined to think they promised her they wouldn't attack me to get her to draw me out. They acted cool with her, with me, and used a type of bait they suspected would hook me right in. They were right. They knew enough about me, about my vulnerabilities and weaknesses, to know how to get me isolated.

How many people have been murdered in such a way? They could have easily shot and killed me out there. I was lucky that they were just stupid assholes and not killers.

Sometime within the next year or so, I was at a local carnival walking around and trying to enjoy myself and maybe meet some friends. Some guys, completely unrelated to the two in the story I just told, came up to me and said, *"Hey, Freeborn, this girl over there wants to meet you. Go talk to her!"* Sure enough, way over there, away from the crowds and by the edge of the woods, was a cute girl waving at me. Now, I knew these assholes were up to no good and wanted to draw me away from the crowds. I had no idea who that girl was.

I declined, *"I'm not interested, thanks." "Come on, man! She's hot, and she totally wants to meet you!"* they replied. *"Tell her to come over here and talk to me if she wants to meet me so bad.*" Understanding that I was in some danger, I made my way out of there and ghosted from the scene completely. I did so by moving into the carnival crowd and staying there long enough for their attention to be drawn elsewhere. Then I simply *floated* out between some rides, careful not to use established exits as I left in the shadows.

Despite what you may think, I had not done anything personally to any of these guys. They decided, for whatever reason, that they did not like me. Part of it could have been due to my reputation by that time as being a fighter, and that put a price on my head. Or maybe I dated a girl one of them liked; I had a knack for that as well. It's all I can figure that would drive any of those assholes to do that.

The point is that I didn't fall for that a second time. I had learned. They may have turned out to be insignificant teenage incidents, but the results were that my instincts were correctly tuned in. My intuition was more completely developed. My orientation was much better suited to such events, and my decision-making process was better informed. I was learning and adapting. Unfortunately, it didn't mean that I wouldn't fall for deception and misdirection later; it just meant that the deceivers would have to be that much better at it to get to me. When I landed in prison several years later, I was *hip to the game,* as we used to say, and juvenile practice runs like that proved to be beneficial as the stakes became higher later in life.

3:7 Orientation drives intuition

Although we have instincts arguably developed over tens of thousands of years, experience is the active feed into our intuition. Our ability to recognize and understand situations, people and events largely comes from what we have seen, participated in and learned. We don't have to consciously remember these experiences; they can be collected unconsciously throughout life. But they are there, nonetheless, guiding our decision-making process at all levels.

Culture also has a great impact on our intuition and instincts. I witnessed this in prison when I would see people who come from quieter, less aggressive environments who would then have difficulties adjusting to their new, considerably more hostile environment. People who come from rougher backgrounds tend to be louder, more social, and more aggressive in general. Of course, this is not *absolute*. Still, in general, it can be true, especially when talking about the criminal element from these areas in particular (which is obviously what you have in prison).

I observed almost unfailingly the acclimation process that would take place for the less aggressive guys' intuitions about danger. Where they came from, the loud, aggressive voices meant something different. It often denoted some type of potential conflict or danger. Sure, everyone gets loud around a sports game or a good party, but to be loud at all times every day? That's not normal for them. You could visibly see their intuitive radar blasting off all day long, seeing a potential threat in every movement, every loud voice or noise, every card game that gets rowdy with screaming and cussing. Those noises are the norm for life in prison. Those poor guys' nerves!

The cultural difference was tremendous, and their experiences in their own culture led them to be alarmed by the behavior of the dominant culture inside the prison environment. Typically, after a few months, they re-acclimated and became accustomed to the new norms they lived in. But during that time of adjustment, their intuition was *not* trustworthy to be accurate in differentiating between actual threats and playful or at least non-threatening behaviors.

I have witnessed the exact same "culture shock" to instincts and intuitions in newer police officers who, coming out of the suburbs or rural areas, get sent into the inner city on patrol for the first time and have a hard time accurately reading the terrain and behaviors of the environment. I am sure this is also exactly what happens to soldiers in foreign lands as they move through the local populations. In all of these situations, your abilities to read a situation and people, both consciously and unconsciously, are hindered by your lack of experience with such a culture.

This is an important fact to think about. Yes, your "gut feelings" are usually correct. Still, sometimes there are cultural differences that you can not understand, consciously or unconsciously, and that lack of understanding causes your default warning systems to fire off automatically. Having the ability to know when it is happening and learn how to function around the unfamiliar is the only way to navigate through it.

We can then understand how our orientation is the primary driving force to our intuition. We can also make the leap to assuming that our intuition is a working component of our implicit guidance system. Surely, it's not a stretch of the imagination to think that our culture, our experiences and our collected information will drive our decision-making, both consciously and unconsciously.

3:8 Fingerspitzengefuehl

Fingerspitzengefuehl is a German term with multiple meanings, all of which apply in context here. It translates to "fingertips feeling." It means tact, diplomacy, and a certain amount of sensitivity to others' feelings in a social context. The minute you read the word "sensitivity," it probably gave you a warm, fuzzy feeling. But sensitivity doesn't necessarily mean compassion. Successful predators, I would argue, maintain some of the highest levels of sensitivity to others' feelings that you will see practiced. Being sensitive to situations, cultural nuances, and individual feelings is the only way to accurately read an environment, group of people or an individual. How you use that information is then up to you.

How this applies in the context of confrontation, conflict and violence comes from the military understanding of strategy and intuition. It involves maintaining a real-time estimate of the battlefield, applying everything we have learned about us, the environment, and the enemy to understand what is happening and use all of that information synthesized into the ability to strategically predict what is going to happen.

The formula to develop this skillset to its highest level is to learn as much as possible about our own and other people's experiences in the space that we are interested in. For example, suppose we are talking about violence. In that case, we have to look at our own experience and confidence within it and the experience, reactions, and cultural inputs of others' lives regarding their perception of violence and their role in it. According to Boyd (from *Strategic Game*):

"We can't just look at our own personal experiences or use the same mental recipes over and over again; we've got to look at other disciplines and activities and relate or connect them to what we know from our experiences and the strategic world we live in.

If we can do this, we will be able to surface new repertoires and (hopefully) develop a Fingerspitzengefühl for folding our adversaries back inside themselves, morally-mentally-physically—so that they can neither appreciate nor cope with what's happening—without suffering the same fate ourselves."

In a letter from Chuck Spinney to Chet Richards, from Chet's blog East of New (*The Power of Fingerspitzengefühl*), Chuck discusses his view on this term and Boyd's take on it:

"Essentially, as I came to understand it (or at least the way Boyd understood it and explained it to me), the word conveys a general summing of a fluid situation by continually probing and testing the environment. It is a synthesis (as opposed to an analysis) of the situation if you will, and it becomes implicit or buried in one's Orientation to that situation. It enables one to intuitively and quickly understand the flow of Observations flowing into and subtly changing the Orientation..."

This intuitive understanding and rapid decision-making comes from learning and experience. Not just "inside of the box" learning, but "outside of the box" learning (which is much more important here). It requires the ability to go outside of the given subject matter, look into other disciplines, fields, and individuals and cultures outside of what you fully expect to encounter. It involves studying the crossing information at the learning point where seemingly unrelated fields intersect and new ideas and new repertoires surface.

The more you understand about a particular target or opponent, the better you can deal with and even predict their strategies and decisions. But the better you understand human beings and human nature in general, the better you will be when dealing with any and all human interactions within your scope of practice, including a particular type of culture.

Look at it this way. If all you ever did was spend time around and interact with people of your own homogenous culture, your ability to understand and communicate with people of different cultures would be seriously hindered. So, what does an experience like prison do for the felon? It exposes him to different races and ethnicities and their respective cultures. It allows him to learn how to interact with whites, Hispanics, blacks, and others. But prison does something much more than that. It will enable the observer to see the reactions of different cultures and the different types of people within a wide range of those cultures and how they specifically react to stress, pressure, and threats to their safety. This is very important information when it is processed into the mind of a predator.

It also allows him to see a side of humanity that most average people in the U.S. will never see directly. The dark, depraved, violent and merciless side of human beings can be brought out under various circumstances. This is shocking information to a brain that has never encountered such behaviors in people; it is literally a paradigm-shifting experience. War also has this effect on those who it affects directly with experience.

This information gives the predator a deep and vast look into the hearts and minds of humans. It fosters a true "fingertips feel" for dealing with people regardless of their backgrounds and culture. It allows for the observation of common behaviors and characteristics, common attachments and desires, across the board for use in human interactions, both social and predatory. They understand what makes men break. They know how to *probe and test*, giving them the power to *fold their adversaries back inside themselves* through prediction, manipulation and domination.

Information and experience alter and shape orientation, and orientation drives intuition. This is how implicit guidance and mental rapidity are developed.

3:9 The Fieldcraft of Perception Management and Impression Management

Impression management is basically controlling or attempting to control how someone perceives you, and it is a component of perception management as a whole. It is something most of us see every day on social media. Since social media allows the opportunity to completely shape and curate 100% of what people see about you, you are free to present yourself in whatever way you wish. Whether it is an accurate representation of who you really are or not does not matter to that audience because they only have this one source of information about you. But doing it in person and in real social settings is much more difficult, especially if you did not have the aid of social media setting the stage for your big act.

Mark R. Leary outlines impression management quite well in the *International Encyclopedia of the Social & Behavioral Sciences* (2001):

"People are more motivated to control how others perceived them when they believe that their public images are relevant to the attainment of desired goals, the goals for which their impressions are relevant are valuable, and a discrepancy exists between how they want to be perceived and how other people perceive them. When people are motivated to manage their impressions, the impressions that they try to convey are influenced by the roles that they occupy and the norms in the social context, the values of the individuals whose perceptions are of concern, how they think they are currently perceived, their self-concepts, and their desired and undesired selves."

I have watched this activity be honed to high levels among convicts in prison. This is literally the foundation of everything it takes to become a classic con-man. It is also a mandatory predatory skill for any dangerous person who hunts for victims in social settings. As I outlined in Violence of Mind, Ted Bundy and his use of charm and victimhood is just one example. Undercover narcotics and gang unit officers are another one to give examples from both sides of the issue.

Social media gave us the biggest explosion ever of both self-made successful people and con artists, both. The use of these new tools allows people to build "credentials" artificially and in completely controlled settings and then leverage those "credentials" into real social settings and businesses. I'll give you an example of how social media is used to create an impression, and then that impression is capitalized on in real social settings.

I have watched many people come and go for over a decade in the gun training community online. Some became famous very quickly and were found out to be untruthful in some of their credentials, if not outright frauds. Others took a long time to build a following, stayed smaller but lasted much longer. But there is a basic formula for making your way into the community at surprisingly high levels.

First, you begin establishing yourself in the online forums, pages and networks. You listen closely to what the "popular" people are pushing in terms of equipment and gear, training methods and tactics, and also for who is acceptable to follow for guidance. Joining that *groupthink*, you embed yourself in the network and begin to parrot the popular consensus on all topics.

At this point, you should be gathering the requisite equipment that the popular network pushes. The right type of gun with the right mods and optic, the popular holster, and maybe even the sunglasses, ear protection, medical gear and clothing to round out *the uniform* of the tribe.

Next, you master the basic skills that will garner you attention and recognition as an accomplished shooter. This could be scoring above a 90 on a 25 yard B8 target, shooting a Bill Drill in 1.5 seconds, having a first shot on target at 7 yards from a draw in 1 second, earning a high ranking in shooting sports such as USPSA, and so forth. Show these skills on social media and specifically within the network and push for that acceptance as not just a shooter but a *very respectable* shooter.

You now have what you need to venture out and begin moving around in real social settings within the network. With the tools, clothing and other props, as well as the terminology, vocabulary and the exhibition skills to "back it up," you can now practice behavioral modeling (also known as behavior matching) to blend completely in with the network. If it looks like a duck *and* walks like a duck...

By attending classes, being a "humble student" but performing extremely well, attending popular events and training summits and getting to know the people you spend so much time with online, you are allowing them to put a face to your name now. A "face" that you have carefully cultivated over time. Maybe you create a YouTube channel, a podcast and even start a local training company teaching beginners and other locals how to carry and shoot. You use the leverage of being socially accepted by the popular network to push yourself out there.

You've made it; you are "accepted" as not only a member of the club, the social network but even have some level of perceived authority to speak on topics important to the network.

What happens next is up to the individual, and I have watched this exact process happen step-by-step for people who have gone on to become fairly well-known instructors and a few who even landed traveling gigs.

What separates the legitimate people working to better themselves from the con-man is a few important things: Is the whole presentation based on *any* lies? How much have they reinvented themselves, and how far is their presentation from who they actually are? What ends up being their ultimate goal at the end of it?

A few examples come to mind of people who were ostracized from the industry for stolen valor, claiming they had military careers that they never actually had. Other imposters are a little harder to detect because they don't technically lie about their credentials. Still, they eventually take on an elitist mentality, which usually lends to them veering out of their lane. An example would be the competition shooting instructor who has never been in lethal fights, in combat, or in law enforcement, who begins telling people, even experienced people, how *real fights* work. That's a big problem, and it happens all the time.

Those are relatively benign examples of impression management, but you can transpose that formula over to literally any other industry or activity. It works the same way. It is literally the formula for social network hacking and infiltration used by corporate spies, special operations units and undercover law enforcement. Read some of the many stories of ATF agents who infiltrated 1%er motorcycle clubs, and you will see the exact same tactics and behaviors used by criminals but only now employed "in the name of the law." You'll see how they used concealment, probing, cue management, deception and misdirection to gain their positioning. You will also learn how they acted as predators and hunted down the weakest links in the pack, isolating them and creating situations to manage their perception and turn them into informants with "no other way out." It's all the same, every bit of it.

Now, let's talk about some outright malicious uses of impression management.

3:10 Prison

Contrary to popular belief that it's all violence and rape, the majority of predatory behaviors in prisons are centered around intimidation, manipulation and deceit. (This also includes the treatment from some of the guards, who often have their own cruel tendencies and behaviors that they live out inside of a temporary and controlled environment, yet another example refuting those who claim our nature is not to be cruel and want to harm or kill one another.)

To illustrate this, I'll explain one of the most common ways that I watched guys get into serious trouble. When you first land in your parent institution, the prison you are slated to serve out your sentence, you arrive with nothing. You haven't had the opportunity to purchase from a commissary or accumulate any goods, groceries, or possessions. This includes basic items like soap, shampoo, toothpaste, etc. You are at the mercy of the state, and they will provide you with their horrible complimentary state products. They really suck.

You have no food, no snacks, no drinks, no tobacco (if any prisons still allow that). Other prisoners know this, and they know many will be in need and want to have these things as soon as possible. They also know something that most new prisoners do not know, it takes a minimum of a few weeks for ANY money to be added to your account.

In prison, there are basically two ways to have money on your account: someone sends the prison checks in your name, or you get paid by the state for a "job." (The prison I was in paid roughly 0.66 per eight-hour day of work, exactly twenty dollars per month for a full-time job.) In either case, it takes several weeks for you to actually have access to your money to spend at the commissary to buy necessities and wants.

The way predators use this information is to manipulate the new person into taking a "favor" from them, a "friendly" loan of some soap, snacks, or coffee. In a flashing moment of kindness and friendship, they will even say, *"Just pay me back on store day."* The new guy may get on the phone to his family and tell them, *"Wow, people are pretty cool here, actually…"*

The experienced con-man knows that it will be impossible for that person to pay them back on the next store day. The money will NOT be there for him to access. This is where the game starts. *"Man, I went down there to get your stuff and my stuff, and they said I have no money!"* to which the predator replies, *"Ah man, it's all good, but I gotta tax you a little, though. Just give me 2-for-1 when you go next week."*

A $12 debt just became a $24 debt. The new guy feels a little fucked, but goes along with it. What choice does he have now? He's a stranger in a new place with no real friends and no one he can trust. He has to navigate this situation, and he has not been acclimated to his environment. He does not know the rules. He's learning the hard way now.

As the predator knew would happen the following week, the new guy still does not have money on his account. It's only been two weeks, and he is now in debt for $48 because it again doubled into 2-for-1 on the previous debt of $24. By the third store day, if he's lucky, he will have $50 on his account to be able to spend the weekly store limit of $50, which means he'll have maybe $2 to spend on himself. In the best-case scenario, he'll have to go back to the well and borrow again to get through the week, and this time it will be 2-for-1 or 3-for-5 right from the start.

But the worst-case scenario, which I have witnessed many times, is by the fourth store day, the victim is now in debt for between $75 to $100, and there is no possible way for them to pay it back because the store limits spending to $50 weekly. At a 2-for-1 rate, they will never catch up. Now they are under leverage by the predator. A few things can happen here, and it is up to what the predator wants and what he reads on the victim.

This can lead to the victim becoming a servant of the predator - from doing their laundry to performing illegal activities that the predator doesn't want to risk doing himself.

It can also lead to violent intimidation to extort more money from the victim. The predator can force the victim to get their families to send money to specific addressees in the prison to save them from the threat of violent beatings, stabbings, or murder.

And in the worst of all possible scenarios, when the victim has no one outside to help him, and he does not have the orientation to face the heat and fight for himself, he can be intimidated into being sexually "turned out" to pay off his debt and keep from being violently raped or murdered. Often, they would from there on out be homosexual and end up being passed around from inmate to inmate for the duration of their sentence. The weakest kids always went that way, and it was a very sad thing to watch, something I had to witness too many times to ever forget.

In the above examples, it's hard to relay to the reader the extremely savvy and cunning manner in which the predator uses impression management and exploits the victim's lack of orientation. The victim lacks the culture, experience and values, all the things that would lead them to better grasp their surroundings and the dangerousness they were in the midst of. They most often come from families and neighborhoods that are removed from this violent and cruel world. They are not prepared to discern threats, nor are they capable of answering the challenge by having the will to fight or to die defending themselves. The saddest fact is, very often, that willingness to fight would be all it would have taken to save them from such a fate.

The predator uses their knowledge of the environment and the culture and exploits their victim's lack of knowledge of the same, and they do so in the very construction of their impression management. You need a friend? *"I'm your friend!"* You need some help? *"I am here for you."*

This same formula is used by predators everywhere. Although I have never been in the military or to the Middle East, it's not hard to figure out the process of manipulation and deception that went into a local soldier being accepted by U.S. forces as a "friendly," gaining access to a military base or installation and then bombing or shooting at U.S. soldiers from within it. It's the same situation for the serial killers and sexual predators. Impression management is an art that predators of every variation employ.

3:11 Effectively Dealing With Impression Management.

One definite way of detecting when someone is running impression management on you is to see them in their natural, relaxed environment. If you see a person in their home, on their property, around their family, you get to look behind the veil. The problem is that most will never let you see that far in, and in most cases where it is high-stakes, the suspected individual will be a stranger, and you will only have what you are seeing in the situation at hand to go on.

However, there are moments (and techniques to create these moments) when you can observe someone in a relaxed state, when they feel like they are in control and their plan is working. This will allow you to see a change in behavior when someone is questioned, their lies are in danger of being uncovered, or they begin to feel like their plan may fail. These feelings will cause some changes in behavior. While there are no standard cues for detecting a lie (despite what elementary-minded people will tell you about twitchy eyes or touching hair), a definite change in behavior is a cue in itself.

This is where counter-management and concealment come into play. When you make decisions about how to act or what to say while in these tense situations, you have to consider it from a few angles:

- What do *you* think about what is happening?
- What would *the person you want him to believe you are,* think about what is happening?
- What does *the person trying to fool you* think about what is happening?

What do you think about what is happening?

You have to know this first, and this information is for you only, at least initially. It is important to acknowledge this angle because it allows us to choose what we show about what we think. A great majority of people show immediate reactions to what they think through verbal and non-verbal behavior. This gives away what you are thinking. By understanding first how you see the situation, you can begin to make clear decisions based on your mission and objectives. This gives you the power to then shape and curate what you show the other person and ultimately what you lead them on to believe you are thinking.

This is critical in a game of deception where someone is trying to deceive you. You have to counter-deceive them into thinking whatever would be advantageous to you at the moment. Sometimes that is just playing dumb and letting them think their deception is working; other times, it may be something else. But the key is first to acknowledge what you are really thinking to yourself and then control the flow of information outward by controlling your behavior, demeanor, body language and words.

What would the person that you want him to believe you are think about what is happening?

The next step is, who is the person he thinks you are, and what would that person think? This is classic deception and concealment being used in perception management. They think they can run this game on you because they take you for a certain type of person. Are they accurate? Can you morph into something different? Can you play along to gain an advantage?

In the game of poker, not letting any of your opponents know what you are thinking is the most widely known aspect. Even non-poker players understand "poker face". It's first not letting any signals out that you are not in control of, being hard to read.

The next step beyond poker face is deception, a deeper level of the fieldcraft of concealment. You are managing their perception of you, and in doing so, not only are you concealing what you really are thinking, but you are also creating a false perception in their mind of what they think you may be thinking. You do not want them to see who you really are. You want them to see someone who thinks slightly differently or has a different agenda. This could be for a multitude of reasons.

Say, for example, you want to buy a particular car from someone. You want them to see you as a buyer, but not as someone who desperately wants *that particular car*, like you just *have to have it*. That would put you at a disadvantage because they know how badly you want something they have, so that they will stick to the highest price, betting on your desire.

Instead, you appear mildly interested but not at the asking price. You show a willingness to buy, to give him what he wants right now-- your money--but also show a willingness to walk away from the deal. You don't *need* his car. This well-known negotiation tactic is used everyday in transactions all over the world. You really think that you want the car. The *person that you want him to think you are* could walk away and live without it. Very often, it is effective.

In a dangerous situation, this same method can be employed in innumerable ways. You may want a potential attacker to think you are unaware of his intentions to catch him completely off guard by giving him the confidence that you are an oblivious target. Still, you pivot the fight by being one step ahead of him when he makes his move.

I recently observed this very move in a surveillance video from a doorbell camera on a private home. The family moved up the front walkway and entered the home through the front door, with women and children going in first while the male brought up the group's rear. As the male approached the door, he didn't make any eye contact to his left or make any overt moves, but when he reached the porch's enclosure, he surreptitiously drew his gun, as is seen in the video. No one else is visible in the video at this point, and he is not overtly looking in any direction away from the door. He completely concealed his draw and actions around the draw from anyone to his sides or rear.

As he spins around, you see an armed attacker explode from his left, and he immediately engages him with gunfire. He won that fight quickly and kept his family safe. Why would he choose to appear to be the guy who was oblivious when he clearly saw the attacker in the bushes but chose not to react right then and there? Well, there are a multitude of reasons. First, if he reacted too early, he would force the attacker to launch his attack, and the intended victim would be in the reactionary position, not in a good position in a close gunfight. He would also be pushing the fight to happen while his family was still outside of the house and directly exposed to gunfire.

He chose not to react, to let the attacker think he did not see him, but to begin making preparations to fight during that gifted window of time where he had knowledge that the attacker was not aware of. He managed the attacker's impression and perception of him and *created a person that he wanted the attacker to think he was*: an unaware victim. As Sun Tzu put it, the man made sure to "accord deceptively with the enemy's intentions." (Art of War, Ch 11) That is who the attacker thought he was, and he let him think it. This allowed him both the time to prepare and secure his family and also the surprise of violence of action when he spins and overwhelms the attacker with way more force than the attacker was prepared for. This is literally what every great strategist has talked about since the dawn of martial tactics.

What does the person trying to fool you think about what is happening?

It's also important to understand this from the predator's perspective. To get close to someone, a human predator will often employ one of several strategies to appear to be someone he or she is not. The attacker can appear harmless, smile, use social norms or exploit your social courtesies to get inside of your space. They can plan this over longer periods of time and use strategies to gain your trust over a period of days, weeks, or months.

In the above example of the guy being attacked at his front door, the attacker believed that he had the element of surprise. He thought he was in control, and the plan that played out would be *his* plan. That's great information to understand because it allows you to shape your projection around his plan and the story he is telling himself. You can essentially begin to shape his world without him knowing it, or you can *plan* to reshape his world when the time is right. This again brings us back to uncertainty and negative images and how powerful it is to use it against your opponent. When an attacker is fully convinced that they have an undetected and foolproof plan, and you suddenly and decisively disrupt and destroy that plan, they are thrust into the reactionary condition, and their confidence, adaptability and agility are put under the greatest pressure.

By framing the decision in this way in your mind, you can manage your own impression to lead him into the behavior you would like to observe. On the simplest level, if he thinks you are totally falling for it, he has the highest chance of relaxing. That allows you to establish a baseline from which to judge his behavior.

It also allows you to cause an abrupt shift in perception and suddenly put him on the spot, causing a sudden shift in behavior. None of which tells you anything specific. Again, it's no science, but what it does is allow you to maintain control and gather information.

An excellent example of this is someone trying to befriend you in prison, especially if you're new there. Now, there are two types of people that try to get close to you in prison, someone who genuinely wants to hang out with you and someone who wants to take advantage of you (or hurt you) in some way. Chances are, it will be the latter of the two. Your job is to determine which one you have on your hands and not cause unnecessary social conflict during the process, and I outlined to you earlier how badly that can go if you are wrong.

I am sure that this exact dilemma applies to soldiers dealing with locals in foreign countries and law enforcement when dealing with locals and suspects. It applies to the woman getting hit on at the bar or the grocery store, and it applies to the average guy getting approached at a gas station.

In prison, you will be approached by every type of human predator known to man. It can be a very dangerous proposition, for sure. I have seen young men lose their lives or become victims of sexual molestation as a result of such interactions that started out in seemingly non-threatening ways. If you are not from an environment where you have developed and cultivated an orientation that is equipped to deal with this predatory behavior, your learning curve is terribly high.

The same is true of average people who find themselves dealing with this level of predator in public. And remember, very often, this is the exact same predator. The individual who did this to people in prison often gets out and is now out here roaming about amongst you, your family, and your neighbors. Do not make the mistake of thinking he or she will be immediately recognizable. They don't all have neck tattoos, obvious drug problems or poor hygiene. Sometimes they are incredibly articulate and could blend into nearly any crowd, including professionals.

Now that you have a better idea how to recognize and begin to deal with impression management let's take a look at how to actively employ it ourselves.

3:12 Effectively Employing Impression Management.

Life is not fair and lying is not always bad. These are two truths that you need to become comfortable with. To think of life in terms of fairness and truth-telling is to think we should always treat others how we *want* to be treated, that we should always be fair and equitable with everyone. While this would seem to be an admirable way to live, it will get you taken advantage of or hurt or killed if you encounter the violent predator someday.

The truth is, if you always treat others how you want to be treated, you leave yourself unable to defend yourself or those you care about. You certainly don't want someone to maim or kill you, so why would you think of doing such a thing to another human being? But if you are ever attacked on the street some night or in your home during a home invasion, you likely will have to do those very things. Suppose you sign up for the military and get sent to a war zone or become a law enforcement officer and go on patrol calls. In that case, you likely may face the possibility of having to maim or kill a human being to stop them from hurting or killing you or someone you need to protect.

Knowing this and knowing how important concealment and perception management are, we need to calculate how others perceive us now that we have these other capabilities and intentions. While it is easy to be likeable and blend into society when you never think a violent thought towards others, it becomes more difficult when you have added personal defense (or professional offense) to your capabilities and intentions. You don't want to make average people uncomfortable for no reason. You don't want people to mistake you for being an aggressive, violent person when that is merely one part of your personality, and you don't want to show your hand to a potential adversary and lose the element of surprise. But it often takes over for many reasons.

Impression management begins with the story that we tell ourselves about ourselves and how others perceive us. Many ex-cons and criminals walk around brandishing their violent attitudes and capabilities like a badge of honor. Large muscles, gang tattoos and patches, the clothing and demeanor that say, *"I'm bad news; don't fuck with me."* And then, we see the **exact same behavior** by the good guys, including cops and soldiers. They'll have the tactical clothing, jacked muscles, tattoo sleeves and a demeanor that says, *"I'll fuck you up, don't fuck with me."* To me, they look and feel exactly the same because I believe they are. They just have different motives and different targets, for the most part. But they're both telling themselves a similar story about who they are and what people's impression of them will be.

In this group of both good and bad people--those who defend innocents and those who will attack them--there are two types: the ones who mean it and the ones who want you to think they mean it. In other words, I've seen plenty of *apparently* tough guys fold up and cry when faced with truly terrible violence. Guys who were loud and even obnoxious, big and scary with tattoos and mean looks, yet when faced with someone getting stabbed to death in front of them, they lose control and run screaming for help. I've seen it firsthand with my own eyes. It taught me a lot. It taught me that my impression of them was not representative of what they were realistically capable of being. It taught me to look deeper into a person's character to determine other important factors that should align with the initial impression.

Have I ever seen this person kick someone's ass? Are there verifiable stories of them kicking someone's ass? Have they ever even been in a fight? What is their background? Where have they been? There are plenty of jacked guys covered in tattoos, taking testosterone therapy and driving lifted diesel trucks that have never been in a real fight in their lives and wouldn't know what to do if it *really* came to them one day.

But the average person sees this guy and thinks, *"Wow, I wouldn't mess with him!"* Now, I'm not saying there's anything wrong with being that guy. You'll get some chicks (maybe), and most uninitiated dudes will probably fear you. But I am pointing out that it's a ruse that runs the risk of exposure if real violence shows up.

Conversely, you find yourself someday sitting next to the guy who has obvious gang symbols tattooed across his throat and on his face. He makes you nervous just to be in the same room with him. His actions and demeanor set him apart, and he is definitely dangerous looking. That guy may be a violent felon and gang member with major violence experience—the same sort of look, much different experience and orientation behind it.

Effectively employing impression management requires a deep understanding of all of this, plus the ability to discern and manipulate a few key components. The impression you want to create doesn't rely solely on your own interpretation of what type of person you are (or are trying to make people believe you are). Impressions are based on the other party's perception (not yours), and perception is rooted in our orientation. This means that our perception is influenced by our culture, values, attachments, parameters (internal/external), experience, confidence, your ability to synthesize new information and, again, genetics. As always, this is true for others as well. **You can not truly manage their impression of you successfully if you don't first understand their cultural views and values.**

As an example, you could roll into Daytona Bike Week on your shiny, financed Harley with your tattoos and crisp leather vest and get a warm welcome from a majority of the people there. The attendees of such an event are diverse and there to have fun. It really doesn't matter if you are a "weekend warrior," "lawyer biker," or a patched club member; they are all there to party! You'll blend right in (especially these days).

Now, take that same presentation and walk into one of the side street dive bars where patched club members hang out. If what you are wearing and portraying is not a *lifestyle*, it will be apparent to those who live that *lifestyle*. You will get spotted quite easily. At best, you'll be avoided and mistrusted. At worst, you may get called out and even pressured physically for being an imposter.

This might sound dumb to read here, but this is exactly why when the ATF sends in an undercover to infiltrate a club, they don't roll in with shiny new everything looking like they shopped at the Harley store last weekend on a lawyer's budget. They give them "rough" lifestyles. He's not John the ATF agent; he's Al the machinist. His parents died, and he has no family (simplifying the verification part the club will do). He will have a story that makes sense for someone to end up in that lifestyle. The type of story produces the rough and tumble, hard luck, blue-collar guy who likes to party but is looking for something more in life, somewhere to belong. A family. It has to make sense for him to be there.

By understanding the culture, values, attachments, parameters and experience of the typical club member and the clubs themselves, the agents have been able to infiltrate and even achieve high ranks successfully. They use a mixture of behavior modeling and individualism to create a believable impression that appeals to the culture and values of their target audience.

How is this useful to the average person? I mean, you're not going to be infiltrating South American cartels anytime soon, right? Maybe not, but if you want to manage a situation that arises between you and a potentially dangerous individual someday, that person's impression of you may mean the difference between a deadly fight or everyone walking away unharmed.

I'll give you a great example of a situation that happened to me in a Florida park a few years ago. I was dressed in a stereotypical, suburban Floridian way: bright teal T-shirt, dock shorts and dock shoes with no-show socks. I would have blended right in with any group of affluent coastal Floridians, which also made me look like somewhat of a soft target to a particular individual in the park on that day.

I saw him approaching me as I sat on a bench at the far end of the park, intentionally sitting where there was less traffic. We were kind of isolated (also a clue). When I realized he was coming towards my bench and not passing me, I nonchalantly stood up and nonchalantly walked to the other side of the bench, placing the bench between us. I intentionally did this without really looking at him because I knew he was coming, and I didn't want him to get the impression that I was afraid, but I did need to gain a preemptive position. So, I moved as if I was planning to do that and hadn't really noticed him.

As he got close, I read the face and neck tattoos and knew immediately that I was dealing with a prison gang member. I had dealt with that particular gang in prison for five years and knew their symbols well. I could also tell this kid was capable and maybe a little desperate or hopeless (which can be even more dangerous). I turned to greet him, and I looked him directly in the eyes. This was important because he was choosing to probe my space; he tested my boundaries, so we were well past the point of averting gazes and not issuing challenges. I wasn't seeking to issue a challenge, only to establish a boundary by showing no fear. *"Come into my space; I'm prepared for you"* was the non-verbal message there.

I was carrying a Glock 43 AIWB with a minimalist trigger guard holster. My draw with that setup is on the quick side, and with the bench between us, that may give me the split second I need to land a shot before an attack could find its mark on me. My concealment was very deep, with no printing. It was also very important to not drop any cues at this point that I may be armed, such as tugging or touching my shirt seam, touching my waistband, or holding my hands in a "shooter ready" stance as some people ridiculously teach to do.

He opened with the classic, *"Hey man, you got a cigarette I can get?"* *"I don't smoke, man, sorry,"* I replied. He followed it up, *"Well, you think you got a few dollars so I can get something to eat? I'm fucked up and hungry, man."* I stated back, *"I don't carry any cash, bro."* He kept going, *"Well, can you give me a job or something?"*

I knew now that the questions were getting a bit ridiculous, and he obviously was formulating other ideas and stalling with questions he didn't seriously want an answer to. We were heading in a bad direction with this interaction, so I took control of the conversation and changed his impression of me immediately. *"Where were you locked up at, man?"* I asked him. He looked slightly surprised and answered, *"I was in South Florida. I just got out a few months ago. My mom lives up here, but she ain't helping me out, and I'm fucked up out here."* I decided to open his eyes a little, so I said, *"some of those tats look like you were locked up up north; where you from?"* Now, he's wondering how I know these facts? He's thinking. He's synthesizing this new information with what he thought he knew, his direction may have to change, and he sees it. *"I'm from Philly, man. What you was locked up or something?"*

I replied, *"Yeah, man. I did five years in Ohio. I stabbed a dude a couple dozen times. I get where you're coming from, man."* I'm fairly certain at this point it started making sense to him, my demeanor, my tattoos, the way I positioned myself with the bench between us, the eye contact, it clicked for him and I could see it. At this point, I chose to deescalate the situation and give him an out by showing him respect and treating him like a human being but holding my boundaries like a convict.

We held a conversation for a few minutes, throughout which I never let my guard down whether I showed it or not. It was easy for me to switch back to convict language, verifying my claims with my behavior and knowledge. I had also made some heavy claims to having done extreme violence myself, which was very intentional. I was striking

160

that delicate balance between concealment and revealing my capabilities, creating some level of unpredictable variables for him.

At a certain point, he admitted that he was looking for someone to rob. In his exact words, *"Man, if I gotta lay someone down out here so I can eat, then that's what I gotta do, ya know?"* By this time, I had shifted my role to more of an equal to him (*in his impression of me*), giving him some feeling of autonomy and of being understood. This was more beneficial than becoming adversarial or aggressive (which almost never ends well).

I also gave him a friendly warning by letting him know that there is no future in what he's doing. I know how hard it can be, and I did it without help, too. I told him very clearly that he would pick the wrong person one day and get *got* himself because that's how this ends, death or prison. I was sending him several messages but not treating him like shit in the process.

He eventually walked away, by which time he had totally relaxed and hopefully felt a little better about life after how I treated him. My goal was simple: not to fight him in the park that day. I achieved my goal.

This is why I am very skeptical of classes that teach very regimented steps or processes to dealing with unknown or aggressive people. That situation was very fluid for most of it, and I had to manually manage the impression and perception actively throughout the entire process. There is no list of steps or procedures that are going to work like that. That's fucking fantasy camp. This whole putting your "STAY BACK" hands up thing that I so often see taught just does not typically work well in the wild. I've tried it, believe me. And when you have a temper, and it doesn't work, then you both end up angry, and the situation escalates rapidly. Ask me how I know…

If you need to attend a class for someone to tell you not to turn your back on strangers, and you think that information is top-notch, then I guess you need that class. But this is common sense stuff at that level. What is seriously involved and nuanced is the true fieldcraft of managing

161

the unknown's impression of you and possibly even managing his perception of his entire environment. Sometimes you need to be tough. Sometimes, you need to be compassionate. Sometimes you need to be timid and concealed to set up an overwhelming counter-ambush to an inevitable attack. Sometimes you need to make them think there is more involved than they anticipated, that the environment may hold more variables than they thought. Understanding how the adversary perceives you (and accurately reading and adjusting to the situation) is the mark of a skilled practitioner.

3:13 Perception Management

The difference between impression management and perception management is that in perception management, an actor will attempt to influence your perception of your environment and possibly your entire situation, not just your impression of them. If you go to a restaurant and the waitstaff treats you terribly, you are left with the perception that the entire restaurant is undesirable and unenjoyable. Similarly, how you are treated when you enter an environment can make you feel at ease, welcomed and even happy to be there.

An example of this is a common game run on new, weaker inmates in prison. A manipulator will approach the inmate when he arrives and assure him that no one will mess with him if he hangs with him. He befriends the new inmate and exploits his lack of understanding about the culture and the rules of the environment. But the manipulator is working in concert with another one or two guys, and this is where the "good inmate vs. bad inmate" game happens.

The new guy will be approached by some bad guys, who will "press" him for money or threaten him with violence for some random reason. This causes the new guy to go to his new best friend for help since he promised this wouldn't happen to him. Feigning total concern, the manipulator assures the new guy that he will go and see what's going on and what he can do. He takes off while the new guy stays close to his bunk and officers and sweats out the time while he waits for the news of his fate.

Lo and behold, the manipulator returns, but he has a deep concern on his face. *"Oh man, I don't know what you did, but these guys are fucking pissed at you, man. They really want to fuck you up."*

"Fuck! I didn't even do anything, man! What the fuck? I was minding my own business!" the new guy replies.

"Well, I don't know man, I'm not sure I can even stop them. I can try to reason with them and see what they are willing to do to squash this. Maybe we can get them to back off or something."

Again, the new guy sits on his bunk and sweats it out with even more terror. They give it some time to really let him work on his own mind, to let his fear eat him up and get him primed for *the move*. The bad guys may even walk past his cell a few times, giving him the *mean mug* and threatening him. If they really want to play it up, the manipulator might even act super concerned and pretend he is lacing his shoes up or collecting some weapons *"in case this shit goes down."* New guy is, by this time, completely freaked out and thinks he might even be killed! And he has only been there a week or two...

Eventually, the manipulator returns and he has good news! *"Ok, man, I think I struck a deal with these dudes. They are willing to squash this beef with you if you are willing to pay them for the disrespect. Would you be willing to work a deal if I can get these guys to agree with it?"*

"Yes, of course, whatever it takes, man. I don't want any trouble." new guy inevitably replies.

The manipulator returns a short while later with the deal. *"Ok, man, they are willing to squash this for $50 in groceries on store day. They know you might be short, so you can stretch it out over two store days, but it will be $75 then."*

And there we have it, the ultimate intention of the whole operation: extortion. The new guy almost always capitulates and hands over the groceries (which equals money in prison). The manipulator and the bad guys all split the take and eat good for a week or two. Meanwhile, the new guy goes without and sleeps hungry every night. Maybe he eventually figures out what happened to him; maybe he doesn't. Often, he becomes a regular target after that.

In the above example, you see how the manipulators completely managed the new guy's impression of them and his entire perception of the situation. They controlled how he saw his entire environment. That is perception management, and honestly, that's low-level employment of it for low-level consequences.

When you practice concealment and impression management at higher levels, you are also practicing perception management. You not only want someone to feel comfortable around you, you want them to feel comfortable in their environment. Or maybe you want them to feel uncomfortable or unwelcome. Either way, your clothing, demeanor, tone, body language, visible attention all of it goes into the perception you create for them.

We all are targeted with perception management every day from marketers in every field. When you walk into a nice resort hotel and everything looks grand and beautiful, and the staff treats you like you are special, they are managing your perception so you have a great time and will spend more money with them and go on to tell all of your friends to spend money with them. Advertisers everywhere constantly tell us how our lives would be better, and we would be happier with their products, and that the world would like us better if we had those products. (I would also argue that the mainstream "news" in the U.S. runs a constant manipulative perception management operation on us, and not a positive one, but perhaps that's for another book someday.) This all brings us to the last lesson here on perception management: the dangers of certainty.

3:14 The dichotomy of Certainty

In *Violence of Mind*, I talked extensively about the concept that uncertainty is the enemy of every fighter. Uncertainty is that blank space in your orientation-observation-decision loop. It's white noise in the heat of the moment. Crafty fighters and predators are good at creating uncertainty in their opponents, allowing them to seize control of the conflict and drive decision-making.

But what happens when we are certain, but wrong? As outlined above, there are many ways that someone can manage your perception of them, the environment and even of yourself. This can create certainties that are false and are designed to work against your best interests. Like the inmate manipulated into believing that a group of guys wants to hurt or kill him and there is no way out (except to pay money), you can be led to believe that you are no longer in control of your situation. You are rendered powerless or vulnerable. You are ripe for exploitation. Or you can be led to believe that your desires, things you want badly, can be achieved if you take specific actions.

This is kind of what happens when some marketing agency makes you believe that you really need this new product. Your life will change with this new car. Your friends will love it when you have the latest phone and can do all of the cool things on social media with the newest and best camera and apps ever! If you finally get that big truck, you can show everyone how successful you are. But is it really true? Do we really *need* these things in our lives in the way that we think we do? Or have we been manipulated into perceiving our situation to be actually different than what it really is?

While the consequences of falling for marketing are just becoming poorer and more reliant on material things, the consequences of allowing your perception to be managed by a predator are much,

much worse. Perception management is the tool of high-order predators because they understand the *dichotomy of certainty*.

They intuitively know that uncertainty is the enemy of every actor. They know this because they themselves will fall victim to it if they don't eliminate it from their orientation. Uncertainty is the white noise, the blank space where you do not have confident answers for problems facing you in the moment. They know that uncertainty causes hesitation. It causes visible cues that are often involuntary that alert opponents that you are experiencing problems that you may not have answers for. It shows weakness and vulnerability.

Like the girl in the soon-to-be rapist's car, when he fails to stop at her house as planned to drop her off, uncertainty takes hold. Her nervousness most likely becomes apparent at that moment as well because she will be visibly agitated or fearful, alerting the predator that he has her in a position of uncertainty and vulnerability. But if she develops that uncertainty too early, it could ruin his plan. He will seek to calm her, blow it off like, "Oh, let's ride around for a few more minutes," or something like that.

They understand this because they know that the artificial creation of certainty is a perfect answer to this problem and gives them infinite possibilities to control their target. They know that the dichotomy between certainty and uncertainty makes both of them equally dangerous to the target if the predator is able to manufacture or control either one.

I know this sounds complex and conspiratorial, and sometimes it is. But it really is something that becomes second nature to an experienced predator, or any manipulator for that matter. They see uncertainty; they react. They recognize an opportunity to create certainty; they act. It doesn't really take much conscious thought once one is experienced in looking for behavioral cues and knows how to solicit certain reactions.

3:15 It's Not You, It's Me.

When a manipulator seeks to create certainty in a target, they know that directly and openly convincing or "selling" someone an idea is the least effective way to do it. It alerts the target to the intentions of the manipulator and tells them that the manipulator wants them to feel a certain way about something. The target will ask themselves, *"Why? What are they going to gain from me by changing how I feel about this?"*

This will not create certainty and will often build mistrust immediately. The manipulator knows the golden rule; it's *not you who has to convince me of something; it's me who has to convince myself of it*. They also know that someone who comes on too strong usually has a selfish or hidden desire or agenda behind their mission to convince you of this idea. So, how is this overcome?

By managing the impression and perception of the target fully. Not applying too much pressure, not appearing desperate or full of desire for a specific end. Avoiding all of the behaviors and cues that would alert the target's intuition and instinct. Sometimes it means appearing the opposite of what they feel. For example, if they want you to stay in the car with them, they may appear like it doesn't matter to them if you do or don't. They could even gamble on creating strong certainty in the target by appearing like they'd rather just be dropping you off and heading home, *"but there's this one last thing we should do first…"*

By understanding the target's perspectives, attachments, values and culture they are able to manipulate the situation enough to cause the target to draw their own conclusions through deductive reasoning, which makes the target confident in their conclusions. The target doesn't feel manipulated because they didn't detect pressure or a bias coming from the manipulator. This is as true for complex operations that involve deep conspiracy as it is for simple heat-of-the-moment events like the example in a previous chapter with the man leading his family into the house, seeing an attacker but allowing the attacker to draw the conclusion that the man hasn't seen him yet while he prepares a counter-ambush.

But there's no way that man could have known anything about the perspectives, attachments, values or culture of an unknown attacker hiding in the bushes, could he? Of course, he could! If someone is lying in wait to ambush you from the bushes, we can safely conclude a few things: First, their culture and values are such that they devalue your safety and your life; if not, they would not be willing to attack you, an innocent person. Next, we know that their perception of the environment is one that makes them feel in control, that they have the upper hand, the element of surprise. This could be viewed as a certainty in them since they believed in their dominance enough to proceed with the attack to this point; they obviously viewed themselves as successful in their projections of the event.

Armed with just this information, we would know enough to manipulate him and his perception of the situation, which is exactly what the man in the story had done. By not changing our behavior despite being suddenly alerted to this dangerous threat, we allow the attacker to continue on his planned timeline, which **_we can now predict_**. This puts us in the control position, ready to *head him off at the pass*, as they say. He wants to let us get to the door, get the door opened and then attack while our door is open and our backs are turned to him. That would be the optimum situation for him. We let him think this is happening, usher the family inside while we surreptitiously draw the gun and prepare to turn and surprise the attacker. I have personally witnessed this exact strategy play out in attacks in prison and on the streets. I am certain I have personally employed these techniques in dealing with a detected imminent attack more than once.

An effective way to achieve perception management is by creating the preliminary factors that allow the target to convince themselves of what we want them to think. Don't tell them to be comfortable; allow them to feel comfortable "on their own." Don't tell them to be upset; give them the information you know they will upset *themselves* with. Don't tell them to like you, be likable specifically to the type of person they are. Don't let them know you're on to them, play dumb and let them go where you now know they will go with it.

The more you know about your target, the more in-depth your control over them, the more accurate your subsequent predictions of their actions will be. These same techniques are used on a wide scale by social engineers in corporate marketing, "news" sources, social media and those who have political agendas (But I digress. Again, for another book someday, perhaps...) Once you learn how "game" is run, you will learn to recognize "game" at all levels. Then you can simply say "no." Or, you can employ some of these same methods and turn the game back onto the predator, in whatever form they may be. Remember, we are most vulnerable when we think we are getting what we want. At those moments, be sure to remove emotion and desire from a logical assessment of the situation.

3:16 The Way Forward

I lived and participated in the violent criminal world for 25 years, and I went on to work and train in the various self-defense industries for 20 years after that. I have been a very violent person, and I have spent a lot of time around people much more violent than me. The funny thing is, very few of those individuals were found in the training world. The scariest and most violent people I've ever known were almost always criminally oriented. These are individuals that had two very important components to their experience: they had perpetrated, participated in and been the target of extreme deadly violence, and they primarily operated alone, with no support or team. That second part necessitated the mastery of the soft skills outlined in this book and of the fieldcraft of concealment.

As the training world in the firearms industry has exploded, it has been the returning soldiers, special operations warfighters, and law enforcement officers who have dominated the scene with classes largely populated by civilians looking to learn how to defend themselves against an average threat on the streets or in their homes right here in the U.S.A. What we inevitably end up with is a training industry that is thick with military philosophy and spirit, big on bravery, "science," and technique. (As a side note, I have met more cops that think they know everything than I ever have criminals who think they know everything.)

It is very common to see people spend 100% of their time learning to run guns effectively and quickly. It literally is all they do in their spare time and is the subject of every single post on social media that they make. At best, they will mix in some Brazilian Jiu-Jitsu and powerlifting to round out the skills that make them "hard to kill." It's no wonder since this is the training that is typically pushed by the "SME's" (subject matter experts). Coming from environments where there are teams, squads, units, battalions, and "brothers" to rely on, and where equipment and training is supplied via taxpayer funding, it's easy to see why the SME's push physical skills, techniques and gear to the top of the list.

Let's face it, it's fun, and it's flashy. For many, nothing is as badass as going out and putting on some nice kit and running the hell out of guns with your favorite former special forces operator, Navy SEAL or SWAT guy. That's a big-ticket item for many.

But when you spend some actual time in the criminal world, especially around ultra-violent criminals, you learn that martial skills and weapons make up such a small percentage of what actually makes someone dangerous. It is the mind--the ability to be vicious and cunning, calculating and manipulative--that makes one truly dangerous. It is the predator who sits back and watches a tough guy show all of his cards on social media, all of his guns, his shooting, his BJJ classes, his deadlifting...and thinks, *"Does this guy think he can't be fucked up? Like, does he not realize that all it takes is for some unknown somewhere to make the decision to hunt him, catch him slipping, and dust him off?"*

Maybe they realize it; maybe they don't. But I can tell you if you don't spend an equal or greater amount of time on the concepts I presented in this book, building that *solid* orientation, all the flashy skills in the world won't be able to save you if you become the focus of a cold and calculating individual someday. There are many, many ways you can be hurt, and it is impossible to protect against all of them. Hell, you don't even know all of them. *And you never will.*

Knowledge and Learning

Knowledge comes from both learning and experience, which can be either random or strategic. If your learning does not involve strategy, then your knowledge will likely never be specific or fully developed. Avoid a know-it-all attitude about anything, no matter how much experience you have. Seek to be well-rounded in your learning, understanding and development. If someone has a different viewpoint or reaction than yours, instead of closing your ears and running your mouth, use it as an opportunity to understand other humans and their behaviors better. *"Why would a person react that way?" "What experiences would lead someone to have these viewpoints?" "How can I use this information?"* These are good questions to ask in those situations, just to give a few examples.

Learn outside of your box of interest. Look for the intersection of information and systems among unrelated fields. Understand different types of people and other cultures. To do this, you have to shut down judgment, at least temporarily. Broaden your scope; everything within the human realm is of interest to those who seek to truly understand humans. If you are going to engage in mortal conflict with other humans, understanding them should be your highest priority.

Strength and Fitness

Physical, emotional and mental ruggedness are essential to survival and performance in life. Physical strength and fitness are excellent foundations for all of the types of ruggedness you can develop. Your body is literally the vehicle for your life. It is the manifestation of your physical capabilities in conflict and combat. **Your fitness is the determining factor in how the physiological stresses of life and conflict affect your psychology and decision-making.** Most of all, it is very malleable. You have control over it to a large extent, so building strength and ruggedness into your muscles, tendons, ligaments, joints, and bones WILL transfer over to the mind's ruggedness and the integrity of your decision-making.

You will find that this physical ruggedness will contribute to an overall increase in capabilities and toughness in all aspects of your life. For more on this topic, an excellent book to read is *Tough: Building True Mental, Physical & Emotional Toughness for Success & Fulfillment* by Greg Everett. Greg does an excellent job of breaking down the concept of toughness and how physical, mental and emotional ruggedness can be (and should be) developed simultaneously.

Strength and fitness are direct ways to alter the orientation in the direction of better preparation and ruggedness. I learned this as a teenager on the *weight pile* in prison, and I have never forgotten it. Almost 30 years later, I am still a barbell and strength coach because I fully believe in the power it has to change and *save* your life. Again, just like knowledge and learning, constantly doing random exercises at varying intensities will not yield the best results. Strategy and intelligent analysis in your programming will give you the best results with the fastest and safest delivery. Do not overlook this component.

Life and Positive Experience

Most importantly, do not forget to live your life and be the best version of yourself in all facets that you can. If you become obsessed with your job or with violence and conflict, you will be of less value socially to friends and family. You also have less access to people of different cultures and values because you are one-dimensional and will have a hard time being interested in and being accepted by others outside of your narrow field of view. Such behavior will limit your access to knowledge and experience, not to mention also having the potential to ruin marriages and family bonds.

Self-Control

Having the ability to walk between two worlds, one violent and full of conflict and darkness, the other positive and full of love, family and friends, requires self-control. Self-control is the ultimate goal of anyone who wishes to operate at a high level in any capacity. Self-control keeps you focused when you personally are uninterested, and it keeps you out of trouble when the limitations of your ego or temper are tested. It allows you to penetrate life deeper in every way possible. Self-control is the ultimate mindset, period. Every strong predator knows that self-control is the only way to achieve the highest possible success rate. Why should you be any different?

To extract the full value from any endeavor, be it fighting, communicating, relationships or literally anything else, self-control must be at the top of your priority list.